# *CHINA TRAVELER'S*

# **PHRASE BOOK**

BENNETT LEE  GEREMIE BARMÉ

**EURASIA PRESS**

**CHINA BOOKS & PERIODICALS**

Address inquiries to Eurasia Press,
302 Fifth Avenue, New York, NY 10001

Library of Congress Catalog Card No. 80-66629

Distributed to the trade by China Books & Periodicals,
2929 24th Street, San Francisco, CA 94110.

Distributed in Hong Kong by Panasia Book Distributors Limited,
Tong Chong Street, Quarry Bay, Hong Kong.

ISBN 0-8351-0729-9

MANUFACTURED IN HONG KONG.

# CONTENTS

*About this Book* ..... 9

*Chinese Past & Present* ..... 11

*Pronunciation* ..... 17

    A Guide to *Pinyin* .. 17
    Tones .. 19
    The Pronunciation Column .. 20

*Basic Grammar* ..... 22

*A Note on Chinese Names and Forms of Address* ..... 24

*ESSENTIALS* ..... 27

    Useful Adjectives & Adverbs .. 29      Opposites .. 35
    Common Verbs .. 29      Useful Words .. 38
    Questions .. 31      Numbers .. 39
    Useful Expressions .. 33      Time .. 43

*CUSTOMS & TRAVEL* ..... 49

    Useful Questions & Phrases .. 49
    Customs .. 50
    Travel .. 50

CONTENTS

*MONEY*                                               55

*WEATHER*                                             62

*HOTELS*                                              65

*FOOD & DRINK*                                        73

*COMMUNICATIONS*                                      85
    At the Post Office _ 85
    At the Telegraph Office _ 86
    On the Telephone _ 86

*ENTERTAINMENT*                                       89

*VISITING/SIGHTSEEING*                                93
    Useful Words & Phrases _ 93    Guangzhou _ 99
    Schools _ 95    Beijing _ 100
    Communes _ 96    Shanghai _ 101
    Factories _ 97    Guilin _ 102
    Museums _ 98    Hangzhou _ 103
    Scenic Sites _ 98    Nanjing _ 104

*PROFESSIONS*                                        105

## *SHOPPING* — 109

Shops .. 110
Clothes .. 111
Colors .. 113

Souvenirs .. 114
Hotel Store .. 115
Toiletries .. 117

## *PARTS OF THE BODY* — 118

## *SEEING THE DOCTOR* — 122

## *COMMON SLOGANS & POLITICAL EXPRESSIONS* — 127

## *FAMOUS PEOPLE* — 134

Political .. 134
Historical .. 136
Classical Writers .. 138
Modern Writers & Artists .. 141
Others .. 144

## *WEIGHTS & MEASURES* — 146

Weight Comparison Table .. 147
Distance .. 147
Area .. 147

## *HOLIDAYS & FESTIVALS* — 148

CONTENTS

## *CHRONOLOGY OF CHINESE DYNASTIES & REPUBLICS*    150

## *PLACE NAMES*    153
Geographical Features ... 153
Provinces & Autonomous Regions ...153
Cities & Localities ...155

## *FOR FURTHER READING*    157

# About this Book

The traveler in China often feels intimidated by the mystery and vastness of a country that, in terms of international travel and exchange, is only starting to open up to the world. The "China experience" brings one in touch with a cuisine, history, society, language, and political universe very different from those of anywhere else.

As language is the most direct means of human communication, this book has compiled to provide the China traveler with a different perspective, a deeper feeling for and, perhaps, a closer contact with China. Although this book does not aim at giving the reader a crash course in Chinese, it does attempt to provide useful words, phrases, and even a few hints to travelers, whether they will be in China for a few weeks or for a lengthy stay.

If you will be on a short tour, *China Traveler's Phrase Book* will teach you basic words of courtesy, words for everyday objects, and a range of expressions you will come across during your trip. It will also prove helpful in showing your Chinese hosts that you care enough to learn a little of their language, something always much appreciated. In this way you will be able to have a deeper and more direct form of contact with Chinese people.

**ABOUT THIS BOOK**

If you are a businessman, engineer, scientist, lecturer or technician staying in China for longer periods of time, you will find this book invaluable in giving basic items of vocabulary and sentences that will make everyday life more comfortable and interesting. It may even give you a basis for learning Chinese.

*China Traveler's Phrase Book* will provide a key to one of the many doors that can be opened on the way to understanding China.

B.L. and G.B.

Hong Kong, August 1979

# Chinese Past & Present

The Chinese language has a history of over three thousand years. As a medium of written communication it has the longest unbroken history of any language in the world.

The exact origin of Chinese is still a cause for much debate. Diversity, however, has been a characteristic of the language from the earliest times. Over the centuries this diversity has expressed itself in different styles of writing, words, and dialects, although outside China the impression exists that Chinese writing consists of stylized pictures and that the spoken language has basically only two dialects: Mandarin and Cantonese. Both of these beliefs are untrue.

Chinese writing, although originally consisting of representations of animals, objects and "picture-thoughts" (ideograms), long ago developed beyond this stage. Many words do contain elements of ancient ideographs, but they bear little direct relationship to their original intention. It is as doubtful that a Chinese speaker will think of the word for "horse" (*mǎ*,马) as a stylized picture of a horse on its side (馬) as it is that a speaker of English will contemplate the etymology of "giraffe" when he uses it in everyday speech. Thus, even though it is romantic to think of the written Chinese language as a series of pictures, it is far from the truth.

Dialects are more complex and serious a problem than is usually realized outside China. In southern China (usually regarded as being the region south of the Yangtse River) there are six major dialects, along with numerous local variations and accents that often make communication between neighboring villages impossible. For example, it can be said that for virtually every major region of Guangdong Province there is a local dialect comprehensible only to the natives of that area. The standard dialect of Guangdong, however, is the language spoken in the capital of the province, Guangzhou (Canton), usually called Cantonese in English. Dialects are such a serious problem that regions still have radio stations broadcasting in the local languages for fear that the national language would be incomprehensible. Local officials, when traveling in different areas, often have to use interpreters to make themselves understood. Even some of the country's leaders speak with such heavy local accents as to be nearly incomprehensible to many.

A unified national language is a relatively recent development in the history of Chinese. Following the establishment of the Mongol Yuan Dynasty in the thirteenth century, the new non-Chinese speaking rulers realized the need for a standard tongue through which they could communicate with their Han subjects. Since the northern dialects of Chinese were so similar and spoken by over half the population of the country, the Mongols, whose center of government was also in the north (at Changan, present-day Xian), decided to use the northern dialect as the *lingua franca*. In this way, the northern dialect became the official tongue (*guanhua*; literally, "language of the officials"). During the Ming (1368–1644) and Qing (1644–1911) dynasties, the capital was moved to Beijing (Peking), and the northern dialect with a Peking accent became the language of the rulers and aristocracy. After the founding of the Republic of China in 1912, the Beijing-based northern dialect was again chosen as the national language (*guoyu*) and remained so even when the capital was moved south to Nanjing (Nanking) and later to Chongqing (Chungking). Following the establishment of the People's Republic in 1949, the national language was renamed "standard language" (*putonghua*) and remains the basic unified speech throughout the country. National radio, television, and films all use "standard language." All spellings and pronunciations in this book are of "standard language" (also known as Mandarin outside China).

It is important to note that the word "Chinese" is usually used to refer to the spoken language (regardless of dialect) of the Han people of China, who constitute over 90% of the population. Yet since China is a country with over fifty national minorities with separate cultures and languages, strictly speaking there are more than fifty Chinese languages. Thus, in Chinese, the language of the Han population is often called *hanyu* ("language of the Hans").

As a written language Chinese is as varied and complex as the history of China itself. For over twenty-five centuries Chinese has accumulated a wealth of expressions and forms that provide the main basis for the development of the modern language. Unlike English, which is most innovative and tends to borrow and create new words, Chinese adds new meanings to old words or builds up new word groupings from old words. Compared to most languages, Chinese has relatively few foreign words, and even now borrows words only rarely. Although each character in the Chinese language represents a single sound and meaning, it is incorrect to think that modern Chinese is a monosyllabic language. The written classical language would generally use a single character to represent an object or idea, while the spoken language would use word compounds. For example, the word *yī* (衣), meaning "to dress," "clothing," or "covering," would be meaningful in the written language, yet in speech it would be put into a compound such as *yīfú* (衣服) or *yīshǎng* (衣裳), so as to prevent confusion with one of the dozen or so other words pronounced *yī*. There are still many monosyllabic words in the spoken and written languages, though compound words make up the greater part of everyday vocabulary. Many compounds stretch out beyond two words, such as *diànzǐ jìsuànjī*, the word "computer."

Due to the ancient literary tradition of Chinese, many expressions and words from classical writing have passed into the modern language. This makes for the strong sense of imagery and poetry of Chinese. Such expressions, commonly called "complete phrases" (*chéngyǔ*) or "classical expressions" (*diǎngù*), often consist of four single words. A more literary or indirect way of expressing suspicion or doubt, for example, is to use the phrase "in the melon patch, under the plum tree" (*guātián lǐxià*). This is a shortened form of "when walking in a melon field don't stop to adjust your shoes, when walking under plum trees don't reach up to straighten your cap," which means that if you stop in a melon patch to adjust your shoes someone may think you're planning to steal melons or if you straighten your cap in a plum orchard, people may suspect you're reaching for the fruit. This expression has been in common use since its appearance in *History of the Tang Dynasty*, written over a thousand years ago. Examples of such expressions are numerous and are an enticement to those who come into contact with the Chinese language to delve into Chinese history and literature as well.

Chinese writing in its early stages of development (about 1500 BC) had a strongly pictorial nature. Many words in the early fragments of writing are drawings: examples are: 人 for *rén* ("man," now written as 人 ) and 川 for *chuān* ("river," now written as 川). As writing developed, symbols expressing abstract ideas also began to appear; for example, the word *shang* ("on top, above,"), ⌣ (now written as 上 ) shows a dot above a line in its original form, while the word *xià* ("on the bottom, below"), ⌢ (now written as 下 ) is that of a dot below a curved line. Many such pictorial characters still exist in the modern written language. Picture writing was soon exhausted as a means for written expression and new words (these date from well before the Christian era) combined a sound, or phonetic, element and a symbol, or indicator, of the meaning of the word. Most words in the modern written language are a combination of two or more elements, some related to the sound of the word, some to its meaning, while others have no obvious relationship to either. For example, words in modern Chinese for various kinds of birds usually consist of a symbol for the word *niǎo* ("bird"), 鸟 , and a sound element. Thus, the word *jī* ("chicken"), 鷄 , consists of the element for "bird" and sound element (*xī*). Due to the change in pronunciation of words over the centuries, many of the original sound elements lack any apparent connection to present-day pronunciation of a character.

Printed Chinese and written Chinese have also gone through many transformations. Although the ball-point and fountain pens have replaced the brush as the basic writing instrument, brush writing or calligraphy is still much admired and practiced as an art in China. The printed form of words is a stylized script very different from handwriting. Due to the large number of characters and their complex forms, over the past three decades a program to simplify the writing system has been undertaken. As a result, the written language used in mainland China is very different from that used in Taiwan and Hong Kong. Even the direction of printing is different; the older form of placing words vertically from right to left has been replaced, so that the lines are now read horizontally from left to right (like European languages). These changes have facilitated the spread of education and literacy in China. Yet it should be remembered that most Chinese have a reading vocabulary of around three thousand single characters, although many actual words are made up of combinations of single characters. Virtually no one knows all of the 50,000 single-character entries of the *Kangxi Dictionary* (China's *Webster's*).

Today, regardless of dialect, social background, or region, literate Chinese can still communicate with each other in the written language, and the gradual popularization of "standard language" is facilitating a new linguistic unity.

# Pronunciation

■ *A GUIDE TO* PINYIN

The Chinese system of romanization is called *pinyin*.

It transliterates the sound of the language — in this case the national dialect, or *putonghua* — into our alphabet. Although mastery of it will require some listening and practice, the reader should have no trouble getting an adequate grasp of it in a very short time. There are other methods of romanization widely used (e.g., Wade-Giles), but since the visitor to China will be seeing *pinyin* and since it is gaining popularity as the standard system of pronunciation outside of China as well, we will give a brief guide to it here.

Most of the vowels and consonants sound as they would in English. Some of the more difficult ones are:

| | |
|---|---|
| **a** | as in "f*a*r," never as in "fail" |
| **ao** | sounds like the "ow" in "all*ow*" |
| **c** | as the "ts" in "it*s*"; "cao" is thus read "tsao" |
| **ch** | as in "*ch*ip," strongly aspirated |
| **ci** | an aspirated "ts" |
| **g** | always hard, as in "*g*o" |
| **h** | as in "*h*er," strongly aspirated (and slightly guttural) |

| | |
|---|---|
| **i** | as the vowel in "*eat*"; when it follows syllables beginning with "c," "ch," "r," "s," "sh," "z," and "zh," it sounds like the "ir" in "s*ir*" |
| **o** | as the "aw" in "l*aw*" |
| **ou** | rhymes with the "ow" in "l*ow*" |
| **q** | as the "ch" in "*ch*eek," not strongly aspirated |
| **qi** | as the "ch" in "*ch*eese," lightly aspirated |
| **qu** | as in the French "tu," with lips pursed |
| **si** | as in a very strongly aspirated "s" |
| **ü** | as in the French "u" |
| **u** | as in the "oo" in "t*oo*" |
| **x** | a cross between "h" and "s," written in some romanizations as "hs" |
| **z** | as the "ds" in "su*ds*" |
| **zh** | roughly the English "j" |

Chinese is a tonal language, and the difference in tone indicates a difference in meaning. In the *pinyin* system, these tones are indicated by marks above the most important vowel in the syllable. Mandarin Chinese, or *putonghua*, has four basic tones:

— 1st tone (high level): spoken high with the voice neither rising or falling, like a single extended musical note; e.g., *mā* ("mother")

∕ 2nd tone (rising): begins with the voice lower and rising to a 1st tone, making it sound like a question; e.g., *má* ("hemp")

∪ 3rd tone (falling/rising): the voice dips and rises. The dip is low and rather elongated and the rise is somewhat quicker; e.g., *mǎ* ("horse'")

＼ 4th tone (falling): the voice drops from high to low; very abrupt and definite; e.g., *mà* ("to curse")

As Chinese words are usually comprised of two or more syllables together, the tones may vary according to the syllabic combinations. Thus, for example, when two third tones come together, the first third tone becomes a second tone. In this phrase book, such tone alterations have been made and the *pinyin* entries should be pronounced as presented.

There is also a neutral tone, indicated by the symbol (°), which should be pronounced lightly and without emphasis.

**PRONUNCIATION**

The objective of this book is to assist the visitor to China in making him/herself understood and in comprehending some Chinese. To achieve this end, approximate English pronunciations for all words and phrases follow the *pinyin* entries. These are based on the phonemes or sounds available in American English. (If in difficulty, the reader can always show his/her Chinese listener the Chinese characters in order to get the meaning across.)

Hyphenated syllables must be articulated very closely together, syllables separated with a longer dash, a little less so.

Here are some vowel pronunciation tips to assist you in using this phrase book:

| | | |
|---|---|---|
| **ai, aye, eye** | as in | "*eye*" or "b*ye*" |
| **ay** | as in | "g*ay*" or "b*ay*" |
| **ah** | as in | "f*a*ther" |
| **ahn** | as in | "W*an*da" |
| **ahng** | as in | "s*ung*" or "t*ongue*" |
| **ao** | as in | "c*ow*" or "h*ow*" |
| **ing** | as in | "be*ing*" |
| **oh, ou, ow** | as in | "*owe*," "J*oe*," or "r*ow*" |
| **o** | as in | "b*a*lk" or "t*a*lk" |

| **ü** | as in | the French "*tu*" |
| **ung** | as in | "*sung*" or "*hung*" |
| **yo** | as in | "*yo-yo*" |

Words beginning with "dz" such as "*∂zao*" should be pronounced the same as the final "ds" sound in "su*∂ʃ*".

**Basic Grammar**_____

**1**   The declarative sentence always has the word order:

*SUBJECT — VERB — OBJECT*

I am going to China

Wǒ qù Zhōngguó

waw chü joong–gwaw

**2**   The interrogative sentence can be formed by adding *mǎ* at the end, e.g.:

Are you going to China?

Nǐ qù Zhōngguó mǎ?

nee chü joong–gwah mah

**3**   Chinese nouns do not have articles or plurals. Thus, the word *bǐ* can mean pen, the pen, or the pens.

**4**   Verbs are not conjugated, e.g.:

| | | |
|---|---|---|
| I look | wǒ kàn | waw kahn |
| You look | nǐ kàn | nee kahn |
| He looks | tā kàn | tah kahn |

**5** The past tense can be formed by adding the suffix *lě* to the verb, e.g.:

    I looked        wǒ kànlě        waw kahn–luh

**6** To indicate negation, place *bu* in front of the verb, e.g.:

    I'm not looking    wǒ bú kàn        waw boo kahn

For the past tense of the verb, use *méi yǒu*, e.g.:

    I didn't look    wǒ méi yǒu kàn    waw may–yo kahn

(*méi yǒu* is also the negative form of *you*, "to have")

# A Note on Chinese Names and Forms of Address

Unlike English names, Chinese names put the surname first and the given names second. Thus, in the name Sun Zhongshan, Sun is the surname and Zhongshan the given name. Common Chinese surnames are Wang, Li, Zhang, Zhou, Sun, Zhao, and Yang. Given names usually have some meaning, often relating to the place of the person's birth, desirable qualities of character, or the names of relatives or friends. In the name Yang Chenbin, Chenbin literally means "[born] at the seaside in the morning," while Li Quansheng would mean "Li [born at the time of] final victory," indicating the child was born in 1949 when the People's Republic was established.

Surnames are passed on from the father. However, women, upon marriage, do not change their surnames. Thus, Deng Xiaoping's wife is Zhuo Lin and not Deng Lin or Mrs. Deng.

Most Chinese surnames are one word, but there are also a number of double word surnames. For example, Sima, as in Sima Qian, the name of China's greatest classical historian, or Ouyang, as in Ouyang Xiu, a poet and writer of the Song Dynasty.

Given names can be either one word or two. Thus, Bai, as in Li Bai, or Jinxiu, as in Yang Jinxiu, etc.

The most common form of address in China is the word *tóngzhì* ("comrade") (see Essentials). Strangers are always addressed as comrade, the word being put after the surname, if it is known; thus Wang *Tóngzhì* means "Comrade Wang." The word *tóngzhì* is used for members of both sexes.

A person may be addressed by their position rather than name. *Zhuren* ("person in charge") is used instead of Wang *Zhuren* or Wang *Tóngzhì*.

The word *xiānshēng* ("mister," "sir") is now reserved for foreign visitors, as are *taìtaì*/*fūrén* ("Mrs.," "madame") and *xiáojiě* ("Miss"). Sometimes they are used as terms of respect for older people. (Women may be addressed as *xiānshēng*, which also means "teacher" or "respected one.") Guides and people who often come in contact with visitors are used to such forms of address.

Among friends and acquaintances Chinese people often use the words *lǎo* ("old") or *xiǎo* ("little") when addressing each other rather than using given names. *Lǎo* Wang ("Old Wang") would be used by a younger person talking to an older one, either a superior or a friend. *Xiǎo* Wang ("Little Wang") would be used by an older (even by only a few months) person addressing a younger friend or colleague. There are no fixed rules for using these terms; the choice my be due to one's feelings about a person and not any actual age difference.

Given names are usually only used between very close friends, sometimes only one of the words of a double surname being used. Thus, Zhōu Jīnchéng may be called *Xiǎo* Zhōu ("Little Zhou") by his friends and colleagues, Zhōu *Tóngzhì* ("Comrade Zhou") by his superiors or strangers, Jīnchéng by some of his closer friends and Chéng by his wife/girlfriend, intimate friends, or parents. His parents, brothers, and sisters may have a special childhood name for him as well. In the south of China the word *A* (pronounced "áh") is often added to one of the words in a person's name to become the common form of address among friends and colleagues. Nicknames are also very popular, *Dàtóu* ("big head"), *Làjiāo* ("hot pepper"), *Xiáohǔ* ("little tiger") being common ones.

| ENGLISH | PINYIN | PRONUNCIATION | CHARACTERS |
|---|---|---|---|
| **Yes** | shì, shìdě | shir | 是 , 是的 |
| **No, not** | búshì | boo shir | 不是 |
| **None, not any** | méiyǒu | may yo | 没有 |
| **Please…** | qǐng… | ching | 请…… |
| **Thank you** | xièxîe | shee-eh shee-eh | 谢谢 |
| **Don't mention it/ it's nothing** | búxiè/bú kèqi/ bíe kèqi | boo shee-eh/boo kuh–chee/bee-yeh kuh–chee | 不谢 / 不客气 / 别客气 |
| **Sorry** | duìbǔqí | doo-ay boo chee | 对不起 |
| **Hello, how are you** | ní hǎo | nee hao | 你好 |
| **Good morning** | zǎo | dzao | 早 |
| **Goodbye** | zàijiàn | dzai jee-en | 再见 |
| **Welcome** | huānyíng | hwahn–ying | 欢迎 |
| **See you in a while** | yìhuǐr jiàn | yee–hwer jee-en | 一回见 |
| **See you tomorrow** | mìngtīan jiàn | ming–tee-en jee-en | 明天见 |
| **Have a safe journey** | yīlù píng'ān | yee–loo ping–an | 一路平安 |

ESSENTIALS

| ENGLISH | PINYIN | PRONUNCIATION | CHARACTERS |
|---------|--------|---------------|------------|
| **I, me; my, mine** | wǒ; wǒdě | waw; waw–duh | 我；我的 |
| **You; your, yours** | nǐ; nǐdě | nee; nee–duh | 你；你的 |
| **He/it, she; his/its, her, hers** | tā; tādě | tah; tah–duh | 他；他的 |
| **We, us; our, ours** | wǒměn; wǒměndě | waw–mun; waw–mun–duh | 我们；我们的 |
| **They, them; their, theirs** | tāměn; tāměndě | ta–mun; tah–mun–duh | 他们；他们的 |
| **Mr., sir** | xiānshěng | shee-en shahng | 先生 |
| **Mrs., madame** | taìtai/fūrén | tye–ye/foo–run | 太太 / 夫人 |
| **Miss** | xiáojīe | shee-on jee-yeh | 小姐 |
| **Comrade** | tóngzhì | toong-jir | 同志 |
| **Old** | lǎo | lao | 老 |
| **Young/little** | xiǎo | shee-ow | 小 |
| **Mr. Wang** | Wáng Xiānshěng | wahng shee-en–shahng | 王先生 |
| **Comrade Wang** | Wáng Tòngzhì | wahng toong–jir | 王同志 |
| **Old Wang** | Lǎo Wáng | lao wahng | 老王 |

## USEFUL ADJECTIVES & ADVERBS

| English | Pinyin | Pronunciation | Characters |
|---|---|---|---|
| **Too** | taì | tye | 太 |
| **Very** | hěn | hun | 很 |
| **Good, fine, well** | hǎo | hao | 好 |
| **Quite good, not bad at all** (lit.) | bú cuò | boo–tswaw | 不错 |
| **Very good, very fine, very well** | hén hǎo | hun hao | 很好 |
| **Excellent** | feīcháng hǎo | fay–chahng hao | 非常好 |
| **Okay, alright** | kéyī | kuh–yee | 可以 |
| **So-so, middling** | mámǎhǔhǔ | mah–mah hoo–hoo | 马马虎虎 |
| **Not so good** | bú tài hǎo | boo tye hao | 不太好 |
| **Lousy, terrible** | choù | chou | 臭 |

## COMMON VERBS

| English | Pinyin | Pronunciation | Characters |
|---|---|---|---|
| **Want, must** | yào | yao | 要 |
| **Have** | yǒu | yo | 有 |
| **Go** | qù | chü | 去 |
| **Come** | lái | lye | 来 |

**COMMON VERBS**

| ENGLISH | PINYIN | PRONUNCIATION | CHARACTERS |
|---------|--------|---------------|------------|
| **See, look** | kàn | kahn | 看 |
| **Listen** | tīng | ting | 听 |
| **Speak** | shuō | shwaw | 说 |
| **Write** | xiě | shee-eh | 写 |
| **Know** | zhīdào | jir-dao | 知道 |
| **Learn, study** | xué | shoo-eh | 学 |
| **Buy** | mǎi | my | 买 |
| **Sell** | mài | my | 卖 |
| **Need** | xúyào | shoo–yao | 需要 |
| **Lose** | diū | dee-oh | 丢 |
| **Give** | gěi | gay | 给 |
| **Rest** | xiūxǐ | shee-oh shee | 休息 |
| **Sleep** | shuìjìao | shway–jee-ow | 睡觉 |
| **Get up** | qǐlaí | chee–lye | 起来 |
| **Use** | yòng | yoong | 用 |
| **Like** | xǐhuǎn | shee–hwahn | 喜欢 |
| **Eat** | chī | chir | 吃 |
| **Drink** | hē | huh | 喝 |
| **Get on** | shàng | shahng | 上 |
| **Get off** | xià | shee-ya | 下 |

## QUESTIONS

| ENGLISH | PINYIN | PRONUNCIATION | CHARACTERS |
|---|---|---|---|
| **Who?** | Shéi? | shway | 谁 |
| **Where?** | Nálǐ? Nǎr? | nah-lee, nahr | 哪里? 哪儿? |
| **Where is/are...?** | ...zài nàlǐ/nǎr? | dzai nah–lee/nahr | ……在哪里 / 哪儿? |
| **How much?** **How many?** | duóshǎo? | dwaw shao | 多少? |
| **How much does it cost?** | Duóshǎo qián? | dwaw shao chee-en | 多少钱? |
| **How far?** | duóyuán? | dwaw yoo-ahn | 多运? |
| **How long? (time)** | duójiǔ? | dwaw jee-oh | 多久? |
| **How big?** | duódà? | dwaw dah | 多大? |
| **What?** | Shénmě? | shummah | 什么? |
| **What's this?** | Zhèi shì shénmě? | jay shir shummah | 这是什么? |
| **What's that?** | Nèi shì shénmě? | nay shir shummah | 那是什么? |
| **When?** | Shénmě shíhou? | shummah shir–hoe | 什么时候? |
| **Why?** | Wèishénmě? | way-shummah | 为什么? |
| **What does it mean?** | Shénmě yìsî? | shummah yee–suh | 什么意思 |

| ENGLISH | PINYIN | PRONUNCIATION | CHARACTERS |
|---|---|---|---|
| Have you...? Is there...? | Yǒu méiyǒu...? | yo may–yo | 有没有……? |
| What's the matter? | Zěnmělě? | dzum–muh–luh | 怎么了? |
| How about it? Well...? | Zěnmě yàng? | dzum–muh–yahng | 怎么样? |
| What's going on? | Zěnmě huí shì? | dzum–muh hway shir | 怎么回事? |
| Which one? | Něi yígě? | nay yee–guh | 哪一个? |
| Which ones? | Něi yìxiē? | nay yee–shee-eh | 哪一些? |
| Really? | Shì mǎ? | shir–mah | 是吗? |
| What time is it now? | Xiànzài jídiǎn? | shee-en–dzai jee dee-en | 现在几点 |
| What is this called? | Zhèi jiào shénmě? | jay jee-ow shummah | 这叫什么? |
| What is that called? | Nèi jiào shénmě? | nay jee-ow shummah | 那叫什么? |
| When do we...? | Wǒměn jídiǎn...? | waw–mun jee–dee-en | 我们几点……? |
| Do you under-stand...? | Ní dǒng bù dǒng...? | nee doong, boo–doong | 你懂不懂……? |
| English | Yīngwén | ying–win | 英文 |
| French | Fǎwén | fah–win | 法文 |

| ENGLISH | PINYIN | PRONUNCIATION | CHARACTERS |
|---------|--------|---------------|-----------|
| **Japanese** — | Rìwén | rih–win | 日文 |
| **German** — | Déwén | duh–win | 德文 |
| **Spanish** | Xībānyáwén | shee–ban–yah–win | 西班牙文 |
| **Italian** | Yìdàlìwén | yee–dah–lee–win | 意大利文 |

## USEFUL EXPRESSIONS

| English | Pinyin | Pronunciation | Characters |
|---------|--------|---------------|-----------|
| **I don't know.** | Wǒ bù zhīdào. | waw boo jir–dao | 我不知道 |
| **I'm not sure.** | Wǒ bú qīngchǔ. | waw boo ching–choo | 我不清楚 |
| **I don't understand.** | Wǒ bù míngbǎi. | waw boo ming–bye | 我不明白 |
| **Please come in.** | Qǐng jìn. | ching jeen | 请进 |
| **Please sit down.** | Qǐng zuò. | ching dzwaw | 请坐 |
| **Please wait a moment** | Qǐng nǐ děngyǐděng | ching nee dung–yee–dung | 请你等一等 |
| **I'm tired.** | Wǒ lèilě. | waw lay–luh | 我累了 |
| **I'm lost.** | Wǒ mílùlě. | waw mee loo–luh | 我迷路了 |
| **I'm not feeling well.** | Wǒ bù shūfú. | waw boo shoo–foo | 我不舒服 |

**ESSENTIALS**

| ENGLISH | PINYIN | PRONUNCIATION | CHARACTERS |
|---|---|---|---|
| **Of course, certainly** | dāngrán | dahng–ran | 当然 |
| **There's no problem.** | Meí wèntí. | may win–tee | 没问题 |
| **Whatever you like** | suíbiàn | sway be-en | 随便 |
| **Thanks for your trouble.** | Máfån nǐlě. | mah–fan nee–luh | 麻烦你了 |
| **What is your surname?** | Nǐ guìxìng? | nee gway–shing | 你贵姓? |
| **My surname is…** | Wǒ xìng… | waw shing | 我姓…… |
| **What is your name?** | Nǐ jìao shénmě míngzǐ? | nee jee-ow shummah ming–dzih | 你叫什么名子? |
| **My name is…** | Wǒ jìao… | waw jee-ow | 我叫…… |
| **Don't worry.** | Bú yàojǐn. | boo yao jeen | 不要紧 |
| **No way, impossible.** | Bù xíng. | boo shing | 不行 |
| **I am** | Wǒ shì | waw shir | 我是 |
| **American** | Meǐguó rén | may-gwaw run | 美国人 |
| **Canadian** | Jiānádà rén | jee-ah–nah–dah run | 加拿大人 |
| **British** | Yīngguó rén | ying–gwaw run | 英国人 |

| ENGLISH | PINYIN | PRONUNCIATION | CHARACTERS |
|---|---|---|---|
| **Australian** | Aòdàlìyà rén | ow–dah–lee–ah run | 澳大利亚人 |
| **a New Zealander** | Xīnxīlán rén | sheen–shee–lahn run | 新西兰人 |
| **French** | Fǎguó rén | fah–gwaw run | 法国人 |
| **German** | Déguó rén | duh–gwaw run | 德国人 |
| **Italian** | Yìdàlì rén | yee–dah–lee run | 意大利人 |
| **Japanese** | Rìběn rén | rih–bun run | 日本人 |

## OPPOSITES

| | | | |
|---|---|---|---|
| **Good/bad** | hǎo/huài | hao/hwhy | 好 / 坏 |
| **Easy/difficult** | róngyì/nán | roong–yee/nan | 容易 / 难 |
| **Old/young** | lǎo/niánqīng | lao/nee-en–ching | 老 / 年轻 |
| **Heavy/light** | zhòng/qīng | joong/ching | 重 / 轻 |
| **Dry/wet** | gānzáo/cháoshī | gahn–dzao/chao–shir | 干燥 / 潮湿 |
| **Cheap/expensive** | piányǐ/guì | pee-en–yee/gway | 便宜 / 贵 |
| **Clean/dirty** | gānjìng/zāng | gahn–jing/dzahng | 干净 / 脏 |
| **Quiet/noisy, loud** | ānjìng/chǎonào | an–jing/chao–nao | 安静 / 吵闹 |
| **Rich/poor** | fù/qióng | foo/chee-ong | 富 / 穷 |

**ESSENTIALS**

| ENGLISH | PINYIN | PRONUNCIATION | CHARACTERS |
|---|---|---|---|
| **Hungry/full** | è/bǎo | uh/bao | 饿 / 饱 |
| **Happy/sad** | gāoxǐng/bù gāoxǐng | gao–shing/boo gao–shing | 高兴 / 不高兴 |
| **Old/new** | jiù/xīn | jee-oh/sheen | 旧 / 新 |
| **Bright/dark** | liàng/àn | lee-ahng/an | 亮 / 暗 |
| **Simple/complex** | jiǎndān/fùzá | jee en-dan/foo dzah | 简单 / 复杂 |
| **Interesting/boring** | yǒu yìsī/wúliáo | yo yee-suh/woo-lee-ow | 有意思 / 无聊 |
| **Beautiful/ugly** | hǎokàn/nánkàn | hao–kahn/nan–kahn | 好看 / 难看 |
| **Safe/dangerous** | ānquán/wēixiǎn | an–chwan/way-shee-en | 安全 / 危险 |
| **Ordinary/peculiar** | zhèngcháng/qíguài | juhng–chahng/chee–gwai | 正常 / 奇怪 |
| **Soft/hard** | ruǎn/yìng | roo-an/ying | 软 / 硬 |
| **Strong/weak** | zhuàng/ruò | jew-ahng/roo-waw | 壮 / 弱 |
| **Smart/stupid** | cōngmíng/bèn | tsoong–ming/bun | 聪明 / 笨 |
| **Hot/cold/warm** | rè/lěng/nuǎn | ruh/lung/noo-ahn | 热 / 冷 / 暖 |
| **True/false** | zhēn/jiǎ | juhn/jee-ah | 真 / 假 |
| **Early/late** | zǎo/wǎn | dzao/wahn | 早 / 晚 |
| **Before/now/after** | yǐqián/xiànzài/yǐhòu | yee–chee-en/shee-en-dzai/yee hoe | 以前 / 现在 / 以后 |

**OPPOSITES**

| ENGLISH | PINYIN | PRONUNCIATION | CHARACTERS |
|---------|--------|---------------|------------|
| **Fast/slow** | kuài/màn | kwhy/man | 快 / 慢 |
| **Big/small** | dà/xiǎo | dah/shee-ow | 大 / 小 |
| **Narrow/wide** | zhǎi/kuān | jai/kwahn | 窄 / 宽 |
| **Long/short** | cháng/duǎn | chahng/dwan | 长 / 短 |
| **Thick/thin** | hòu/bó | hoe/baw | 厚 / 薄 |
| **Tall/short** | gāo/ǎi | gao/aye | 高 / 矮 |
| **Fat/lean** | pàng/shòu | pahng/show | 胖 / 瘦 |
| **High/low** | gāo/dī | gao/dee | 高 / 底 |
| **Near/far** | jìn/yuǎn | jeen/yoo-ahn | 近 / 远 |
| **Here/there** | zhèlǐ, zhèr/ nàlǐ, nàr | jelly, jar/nah-lee, nahr | 这里, 这儿 / 那里, 那儿 |
| **Front/back** | qián/hòu | chee-en/hoe | 前 / 后 |
| **Inside/outside** | lǐbiān/wàibiān | lee-bee-en/ why-bee-en | 里边 / 外边 |
| **Under/over** | xiàbiā/shàngbiān | shee-ya-bee-en/ shahng-bee-en | 下边 / 上边 |
| **Left/right** | zuǒ/yòu | dzwaw/yo | 左 / 右 |
| **Empty/full** | kōng/mǎn | koong/man | 空 / 满 |

ESSENTIALS

| ENGLISH | PINYIN | PRONUNCIATION | CHARACTERS |
|---------|--------|---------------|------------|
| **Open/shut** | kāi/guān | kai/gwan | 开 / 关 |
| **Deep/shallow** | shēn/qiǎn | shun/chee-en | 深 / 浅 |
| **Many/few** | duō/shǎo | dwaw/shao | 多 / 少 |
| **First/last** | xiān/hòu | shee-en/hoe | 先 / 后 |

## USEFUL WORDS

| ENGLISH | PINYIN | PRONUNCIATION | CHARACTERS |
|---------|--------|---------------|------------|
| **At** | zài | dzai | 在 |
| **On** | zài…shàng | dzai…shahng | 在……上 |
| **In** | zài…lǐ | dzai…lee | 在……里 |
| **From** | cóng | tsoong | 从 |
| **Toward** | xiàng | shee-ahng | 向 |
| **During** | zài…dě shíhòu | dzai…duh shir–hoe | 在……的时候 |
| **And (with)** | hé/gēn, tóng | huh/gun, toong | 和, 跟, 同 |
| **Or** | háishì | hye–shir | 还是 |
| **Extremely** | fēicháng | fay–chahng | 非常 |
| **Also** | yě | yeh | 也 |
| **Soon** | mǎshàng | mah–shahng | 马上 |
| **Perhaps** | kěnéng | kuh–nung | 可能 |

| ENGLISH | PINYIN | PRONUNCIATION | CHARACTERS |
|---------|--------|---------------|------------|
| **North** | běi | bay | 北 |
| **South** | nán | nan | 南 |
| **East** | dōng | doong | 东 |
| **West** | xī | shee | 西 |

## NUMBERS

| | ENGLISH | PINYIN | PRONUNCIATION | CHARACTERS |
|---|---------|--------|---------------|------------|
| **0** | **zero** | líng | ling | 零, 0 |
| **1** | **one** | yī | yee | 一 |
| **2** | **two** | èr | are | 二 |
| **3** | **three** | sān | san | 三 |
| **4** | **four** | sì | suh | 四 |
| **5** | **five** | wǔ | woo | 五 |
| **6** | **six** | liù | lee-oh | 六 |
| **7** | **seven** | qī | chee | 七 |
| **8** | **eight** | bā | bah | 八 |
| **9** | **nine** | jiǔ | jee-oh | 九 |
| **10** | **ten** | shí | shir | 十 |
| **Eleven** | | shíyī | shir–yee | 十一 |
| **Twelve** | | shí'èr | shir–are | 十二 |

ESSENTIALS

| ENGLISH | PINYIN | PRONUNCIATION | CHARACTERS |
|---|---|---|---|
| **Thirteen** | shísān | shir–san | 十三 |
| **Fourteen** | shí'sì | shir–suh | 十四 |
| **Fifteen** | shíwǔ | shir–woo | 十五 |
| **Sixteen** | shíliù | shir–lee-oh | 十六 |
| **Seventeen** | shíqī | shir–chee | 十七 |
| **Eighteen** | shíbā | shir–bah | 十八 |
| **Nineteen** | shíjiǔ | shir–jee-oh | 十九 |
| | | | |
| **Twenty** | èrshí | are–shir | 二十 |
| **Twenty-one** | èrshíyī | are–shir–yee | 二十一 |
| **Twenty-two** | èrshí'èr | are–shir–are | 二十二 |
| **Twenty-three** | èrshísān | are–shir–san | 二十三 |
| | | | |
| **Thirty** | sānshí | san–shir | 三十 |
| **Forty** | sìshí | suh–shir | 四十 |
| **Fifty** | wǔshí | woo–shir | 五十 |
| | | | |
| **Hundred** | bǎi | bye | 百 |
| **One hundred** | yìbǎi | yee–bye | 一百 |
| **Two hundred** | èrbǎi | are–bye | 二百 |

| *ENGLISH* | *PINYIN* | *PRONUNCIATION* | *CHARACTERS* |
|---|---|---|---|
| **Thousand** | qiān | chee-en | 千 |
| **Six thousand** | liùqiān | lee-oh chee-en | 六千 |
| **Ten thousand** | yíwàn | yee–wahn | 一万 |
| **Million** | bǎiwàn | bye–wahn | 百万 |
| **Forty-four** | sìshísì | suh–shir–suh | 四十四 |
| **Sixty-nine** | liùshíjiǔ | lee-oh–shir–jee-oh | 六十九 |
| **Three hundred twenty** | sānbǎi èrshí | sahn–bye are–shir | 三百二十 |
| **Two thousand seven hundred** | liǎngqiān qībǎi | lee-ahng–chee-en chee–bye | 两千七百 |
| **Ninety-four thousand five hundred eighty-one** | jiǔwàn sìqiān wúbǎi bāshíyī | jee-oh–wahn suh–chee-en woo–bye bah–shir–yee | 九万四千五百八十一 |
| **First** | dìyī | dee–yee | 第一 |
| **Second** | dì'èr | dee–are | 第二 |
| **Third** | dìsān | dee–san | 第三 |
| **Fourth** | dìsì | dee–suh | 第四 |
| **Fifth** | dìwǔ | dee–woo | 第五 |
| **Sixth** | dìliù | dee–lee-oh | 第六 |
| **Seventh** | dìqī | dee–chee | 第七 |

ESSENTIALS

| ENGLISH | PINYIN | PRONUNCIATION | CHARACTERS |
|---------|--------|---------------|------------|
| **Eighth** | dìbā | dee–bah | 第八 |
| **Ninth** | dìjiŭ | dee–jee-oh | 第九 |
| **Tenth** | dìshí | dee–shir | 第十 |
| **Point (decimal)** | diăn | dee-en | 点 |
| **15.07** | shíwŭ diăn líng qī | shir–woo dee-en ling–chee | 十五点○七 |
| **% Percent** | băi fēnzhī… | bye–fun-jir… | 百分之 |
| **33.3%** | băifēnzhī sānshísān diăn sān | bye–fun-jir san–shir–san dee-en san | 百分之三十三点三 |
| **100%** | băifēnzhī băi | bye–fun-jir bye | 百分之百 |
| **¼** | sìfēnzhī yī | suh–fun-jir yee | 四分之一 |
| **¾** | sìfēnzhī sān | suh–fun-jir–san | 四分之三 |
| **⅓** | sānfēnzhī yi | san–fun-jir yee | 三分之一 |
| **⅔** | sānfēnzhī èr | san–fun-jir are | 三分之二 |
| **½** | yíbàn | yee–ban | 一半 |

## TIME

| ENGLISH | PINYIN | PRONUNCIATION | CHARACTERS |
|---|---|---|---|
| **Time (abstract)** | shíjiān | shir–jee-en | 时间 |
| **Time (concrete)** | shíhòu | shir–hoe | 时候 |
| **Clock** | zhōng | joong | 钟 |
| **Watch** | biāo | bee-ow | 表 |
| **O'clock** | diǎnzhōng | dee-en joong | 点钟 |
| **Second** | miǎo | meow | 秒 |
| **Minute** | fēnzhōng | fun–joong | 分钟 |
| **Hour** | xiǎoshí | shee-ow–shir | 小时 |
| **One hour** | yígě xiǎoshí | yee–guh shee-ow–shir | 一个小时 |
| **Two hours** | liǎnggě xiǎoshí | lee-ahng–guh shee-ow–shir | 两个小时 |
| **Half-hour** | bàngě xiǎoshí | bahn–guh shee-ow–shir | 半个小时 |
| **Quarter of an hour** | yíkè zhōng | yee–kuh joong | 一刻钟 |

| ENGLISH | PINYIN | PRONUNCIATION | CHARACTERS |
|---|---|---|---|
| **Now** | xiànzài | shee-en–dzai | 现在 |
| **What time is it now?** | Xiànzài jǐdiǎn (zhōng)? | shee-en–dzai jee dee-en (joong) | 现在几点 (钟)？ |
| **It is now five o'clock.** | Xiànzài wúdiǎn (zhōng). | shee-en–dzai woo–dee-en (joong) | 现在五点 (钟 |
| **Two o'clock** | liángdiǎn (zhōng) | lee-ahng dee-en (joong) | 两点 (钟) |
| **Seven-thirty** | qīdiǎn sānshí (fēn) | chee dee-en san–shir (fun) | 七点三十 (分) |
| **Half past seven** | qīdiǎn bàn | chee dee-en ban | 七点半 |
| **Four-fifteen** | sìdiǎn shíwǔ (fēn) | suh–dee-en shir–woo (fun) | 四点十五 (分) |
| **Quarter past four** | sìdiǎn yíkè | suh–dee-en yee-kuh | 四点一刻 |
| **Twelve forty-five** | shí'èrdiǎn sìshíwǔ | shir–are dee-en suh–shir–woo | 十二点四十五 |
| **Quarter to one** | yìdiǎn chà yíkè | yee–dee-en cha yee–kuh | 一点差一刻 |
| **It's time (to go)** | dào diǎnlė | dao dee-en–luh | 到点了 |

ESSENTIALS

| ENGLISH | PINYIN | PRONUNCIATION | CHARACTERS |
|---------|--------|---------------|------------|
| **Month** | yuè | yweh | 月 |
| **January** | Yīyuè | yee–yweh | 一月 |
| **February** | Èryuè | are–yweh | 二月 |
| **March** | Sānyè | san–yweh | 三月 |
| **April** | Sìyuè | suh–yweh | 四月 |
| **May** | Wǔyuè | woo–yweh | 五月 |
| **June** | Liùyuè | lee-oh–yweh | 六月 |
| **July** | Qīyuè | chee–yweh | 七月 |
| **August** | Bāyuè | bah–yweh | 八月 |
| **September** | Jiǔyuè | jee-oh–yweh | 九月 |
| **October** | Shíyuè | shir–yweh | 十月 |
| **November** | Shíyīyuè | shir–yee–yweh | 十一月 |
| **December** | Shí'èryuè | shir–are–yweh | 十二月 |
| | | | |
| **Year** | nián | nee-en | 年 |
| **This year** | jīnnián | jeen–nee-en | 今年 |
| **Last year** | qùnián | chü–nee-en | 去年 |
| **Next year** | míngnián | ming–nee-en | 明年 |

ESSENTIALS

| ENGLISH | PINYIN | PRONUNCIATION | CHARACTERS |
|---------|--------|---------------|------------|
| **This week** | zhèigě xīngqī | jay–guh shing–chee | 这个星期 |
| **Last week** | shànggě xīngqī | shahng–guh shing–chee | 上个星期 |
| **Next week** | xiàgě xīngqī | shee-ya–guh shing–chee | 下个星期 |
| **This month** | zhèigě yuè | jay–guh yweh | 这个月 |
| **Last month** | shànggě yuè | shahng–guh yweh | 上个月 |
| **Next month** | xiàgě yuè | shee-ya–guh yweh | 下个月 |
| **Season** | jìjié | jee–jee-yeh | 季节 |
| **Spring** | chūntiān | chwin–tee-en | 春天 |
| **Summer** | xiàtiān | shee-ah–tee-en | 夏天 |
| **Autumn** | qiūtiān | chee-oh–tee-en | 秋天 |
| **Winter** | dōngtiān | doong–tee-en | 冬天 |
| **Morning (early)** | zǎoshàng | zao–shahng | 早上 |
| **Morning (forenoon)** | shàngwǔ | shahng–woo | 上午 |
| **Noon** | zhōngwǔ | joong–woo | 中午 |

| ENGLISH | PINYIN | PRONUNCIATION | CHARACTERS |
|---|---|---|---|
| **Afternoon** | xiàwǔ | shee-ya–woo | 下午 |
| **Evening** | wǎnshàng | wahn–shahng | 晚上 |
| **Midnight** | wǔyè, bànwǎn | woo–yeh, ban–wahn | 午夜，半晚 |
| **Daytime** | báitiān | bye–tee-en | 白天 |
| **Nighttime** | yèlǐ, wǎnshàng | yeh–lee, wahn–shahng | 夜里，晚上 |
| **Sunrise** | límíng, rìchū | lee–ming, rih–choo | 黎明，日出 |
| **Sunset** | bàngwǎn, rìluò | bahng–wahn, rih–lwoh | 傍晚，日落 |
| | | | |
| **8:47 A.M.** | shàngwǔ bādiǎn sìshíqī (fēn) | shahng–woo bah–dee-en suh–shir–chee (fun) | 上午八点四十七（分） |
| **3:30 P.M.** | xiàwǔ sāndiǎn sānshí (fēn) | shee-ya–woo san–dee-en san–shir (fun) | 下午三点三十（分） |
| **11:02 P.M.** | wǎnshàng shíyī diǎn língèr (fēn) | wahn–shahng shir–yee dee-en ling–are (fun) | 晚上十一点0二（分） |
| | | | |
| **Day** | tiān | tee-en | 天 |
| **Yesterday** | zuótiān | dzwaw–tee-en | 昨天 |
| **Today** | jīntiān | jeen–tee-en | 今天 |
| **Tomorrow** | míngtiān | ming–tee-en | 明天 |
| **Day before yesterday** | qiántiān | chee-en tee-en | 前天 |

TIME

| ENGLISH | PINYIN | PRONUNCIATION | CHARACTERS |
| --- | --- | --- | --- |
| **Day after tomorrow** | hòutiān | hoe tee-en | 后天 |
| **This afternoon** | jīntiān xiàwǔ | jeen–tee-en shee-ya–woo | 今天下午 |
| **Yesterday evening** | zuótiān wǎnsháng | dzwaw–tee-en wahn–shahng | 昨天晚上 |
| **Tomorrow morning** | míngtiān shàngwǔ | ming–tee-en shahng–woo | 明天上午 |
| | | | |
| **Week** | xīngqī/lǐbài | shing–chee/lee–bye | 星期 / 礼拜 |
| **Sunday** | Xīngqītiān | shing–chee–teen-en | 星期天 |
| **Monday** | Xīngqīyī | shing–chee–yee | 星期一 |
| **Tuesday** | Xīngqī'èr | shing–chee–are | 星期二 |
| **Wednesday** | Xīngqīsān | shing–chee–san | 星期三 |
| **Thursday** | Xīngqīsì | shing–chee–suh | 星期四 |
| **Friday** | Xīngqīwǔ | shing–chee–woo | 星期五 |
| **Saturday** | Xīngqīliù | shing–chee–lee-oh | 星期六 |
| | | | |
| **What day is it today?** | Jīntiān xīngqī jǐ | jeen–tee-en shing–chee jee | 今天星期几? |

| ENGLISH | PINYIN | PRONUNCIATION | CHARACTERS |
|---------|--------|---------------|------------|

## USEFUL QUESTIONS & PHRASES

| ENGLISH | PINYIN | PRONUNCIATION | CHARACTERS |
|---------|--------|---------------|------------|
| **Hello.** | Ní hǎo. | nee hao | 你好 |
| **Thank you.** | Xiè-xiě. | shee-eh shee-eh | 谢谢 |
| **Please help me.** | Qíng nǐ bāngzhù wǒ. | ching nee bahng–jew waw | 请你帮助我 |
| **Where's the toilet?** | Cèsuǒ zài nǎr? | tse–swo dzai nahr | 厕所在哪儿？ |
| **I want to rest.** | Wǒ yào xiūxǐ. | waw yao shee-oh–shee | 我要休息 |
| **I'm tired.** | Wǒ lèilě. | waw lay–luh | 我累了 |
| **How long do I have to wait?** | Yào děng duó jiǔ? | yao dung dwaw dee-oh | 要等多久？ |
| **Is there anyone to meet me?** | Yǒu rén lái jiē wǒ mǎ? | yo run lye jee-yeh waw mah | 有人来接我吗？ |
| **Can I go?** | Kéyǐ zǒu mǎ? | kuh–yee dzou mah | 可以走吗？ |
| **I want a taxi.** | Wǒ yào yígè qìchē. | waw yao yee–guh chee–cheh | 我要一个汽车 |
| **O.K.?** | Hǎo bù hǎo? | hao boo hao | 好不好 |

## CUSTOMS

| ENGLISH | PINYIN | PRONUNCIATION | CHARACTERS |
|---|---|---|---|
| **China International Travel Service (C.T.S.)** | Lǚxíngshè/guòlǚ | lü–shing–shuh/ gwaw–loo | 旅行社 / 国族 |
| **Customs** | hǎiguān | hye–gwan | 海关 |
| **Passport** | hùzhào | hoo–jao | 护照 |
| **Visa** | qiānzhèng | chee–en–juhng | 签证 |
| **Baggage** | xínglǐ | shing–lee | 行李 |
| **Search/inspection** | jiǎnchá | jee-en-cha | 检察 |
| **Exchange money/ bank** | huànqiàn/yínháng | hwahn–chee–en/ yeen–hung | 换钱 / 银行 |
| **(Are you) finished?** | Wán-lě? | wahn–luh | 完了? |

## TRAVEL

| ENGLISH | PINYIN | PRONUNCIATION | CHARACTERS |
|---|---|---|---|
| **Airplane** | fēijī | fay–jee | 飞机 |
| **To fly** | fēi | fay | 飞 |
| **Airport** | fēijīchǎng | fay–jee–chahng | 飞机场 |
| **Go by plane** | zuò fēijī | dzwaw fay–jee | 坐飞机 |

| ENGLISH | PINYIN | PRONUNCIATION | CHARACTERS |
|---------|--------|---------------|------------|
| **Plane ticket** | fēijīpiào | fay–jee pee-ow | 飞机票 |
| **Take off** | qǐfēi | chee–fay | 起飞 |
| **Land** | jiàngluò | jee-ahng–lwaw | 降落 |
| **Where are we?** | Wǒmen zài shénme dìfang? | waw–mun dzai shummah dee-fahng | 我们在什么地方? |
| **We are in...** | Wǒmen zài... | waw–mun dzai | 我们在…… |
| **Tea** | chá | cha | 茶 |
| **Could I have some tea?** | Kéyǐ lái chá mǎ? | kuh–yee lye cha mah | 可以来茶吗? |
| **I don't feel well.** | Wǒ bù shūfú. | waw boo shoo-foo | 我不舒服 |
| **Restroom** | cèsuǒ | tse–swo | 厕所 |
| **Seat** | zuòwèi | dzwaw–way | 坐位 |
| **Seatbelt** | ānquándài | an–chwan–dye | 安全带 |
| **...is broken** | ...huài-le | hwhy–luh | ……坏了 |
| **Train** | huǒchē | hwaw–cheh | 火车 |
| **Soft sleeper (1st class)** | ruǎnwò | roo-an–waw | 软卧 |
| **Hard sleeper (2nd class)** | yìngwò | ying–waw | 硬卧 |
| **Hard seat (3rd class)** | yìngzuò | ying–dzwaw | 硬坐 |

CUSTOMS & TRAVEL

| ENGLISH | PINYIN | PRONUNCIATION | CHARACTERS |
|---------|--------|---------------|------------|
| **Train station** | huǒchēzhàn | hwaw–cheh–jan | 火车站 |
| **Train ticket** | huǒchēpiào | hwaw–cheh–pee-ow | 火车票 |
| **Compartment** | chēxiāng | cheh–shee-ahng | 车厢 |
| **Which...?** | něi yí-gè...? | nay yee–guh | 哪一个……? |
| **Hot water** | kāishuǐ | kye–shway | 开水 |
| **Fan** | diànshàn | dee-en shan | 电扇 |
| **Put on the fan** | kāi diànshàn | kai dee-en shan | 开电扇 |
| **(It's) not working** | ...huài-lě | hwhy–luh | ……坏了 |
| **Pillow** | zhěntóu | jun–toe | 枕头 |
| **Blanket** | tǎnzi / máotǎn | tan–dzih / mao–tan | 毯子 / 毛毯 |
| **Cup** | bēizǐ | bay–dzih | 杯子 |
| **Light** | dēng | dung | 灯 |
| **Loudspeaker** | lǎbǎ | lah–bah | 喇叭 |
| **Music** | yīnyuè | yeen–yweh | 音乐 |
| **Too loud** | tài dàshēng | tye dah–shung | 太大声 |
| **Turn (it) off** | (bǎ tā) guāndiào | (bah tah) gwan–dee-ow | （把它）关掉 |
| **Toilet paper** | wèishēngzhǐ | way–shung jir | 卫生纸 |
| **Do you have any...?** | Yǒu... mǎ? | yo... mah | 有……吗? |

| **Dining car** | cānchē | tsahn–cheh | 餐车 |
| **Knife and fork** | dāochā | dao-cha | 刀叉 |
| **Chopsticks** | kuàizĭ | kwhy–dzih | 筷子 |
| **Beer** | píjiŭ | pee–jee-oh | 啤酒 |
| **Soft drink** | qìshuĭ | chee–shway | 汽水 |
| **Cold** | lĕng | lung | 冷 |

*(For other foods, see "Eating")*

| **Public bus** | gōnggòng qìchē | goong–goong chee–cheh | 公共汽车 |
| **Mini bus** | miànbāo chē | meen-en bao–cheh | 面包车 |
| **Bus ticket** | chēpiào | cheh–pee-ow | 车票 |
| **Bus stop** | chēzhàn | cheh–jan | 车站 |
| **Last stop** | zhōngzhàn | joong–jan | 终站 |
| **... stops** | ... zhàn | ... jan | ……站 |
| **Get on** | shàng chē | shahng–cheh | 上车 |
| **Get off** | xià chē | shee-ya–cheh | 下车 |
| **I want to go to...** | Wŏ yào qù... | waw yao chü | 我要去…… |
| **Stop!** | Tíng! | ting | 停！|
| **You've passed it.** | Yĭjīng guòlĕ. | yee–jing gwaw–luh | 已经过了 |

TRAVEL

| ENGLISH | PINYIN | PRONUNCIATION | CHARACTERS |
|---|---|---|---|
| **How far? (stops)** | Jǐ zhàn? | jee jan | 几站？ |
| **How far is it to...?** | Dào…yǒu duó yuǎn? | dao yo dwaw yoo-ahn | 到……有多远？ |
| **How long? (time)** | Duó jiǔ? | dwaw jee-oh | 多久？ |
| **How much? (money)** | Duóshǎo qián? | dwaw–shao chee-en | 多少钱？ |
| **Where to?** | Dào nálǐ?/nǎr? | dao nah–lee/nahr | 多哪里/哪儿？ |
| **Bus/taxi driver** | sījī | sih–jee | 司机 |
| **Taxi** | chūzū qìchē | choo–dzoo chee–cheh | 出租汽车 |
| **Take me back to the hotel.** | Sòng wǒ huí fàndiàn. | soong waw hway fan–dee-en | 送我回饭店 |
| **Slower** | màn yì diǎn | man yee–dee-en | 慢一点 |
| **Faster** | kuài yì diǎn | kwhy yee–dee-en | 快一点 |
| **(Please) wait** | (qǐng)děng yì děng | (ching) dung–yee-dung | （请）等一等 |
| **Stop for a moment.** | Tíng yí xià. | ting yee–shee-ya | 停一下 |
| **How long will I have to wait?** | Yaò děng duó jiǔ? | yao dung dwaw jee-oh | 要等多久？ |
| **Left/right** | zuǒ/yòu | dzwaw/yo | 左/右 |
| **Straight ahead** | yìzhí zǒu | yee–jir dzou | 一直走 |

Chinese currency is called *renminbi*, which literally means "people's currency." The basic unit of currency is the *yuan*. In speech, the *yuan* is commonly referred to as *kuai*. The *yuan*, or *kuai*, comes in paper notes of 10 *kuai*, 5 *kuai*, 2 *kuai*, and 1 *kuai*. Each *kuai* has one hundred *fen*. Fen comes in coins of 1 *fen*, 2 *fen*, and 5 *fen*. One-tenth of a *yuan*, or 10 *fen*, are a *jiao*, which in speech is commonly called a *mao*. There are paper notes for one-tenth of a *yuan*, or 10 *fen*, called 1 *mao*; for one-fifth of a *yuan*, or twenty *fen*, called 2 *mao*; and for one-half of a *yuan*, or 50 *fen*, called 5 *mao*.

Visitors will be able to change money at the hotel, at the Friendship Stores, at train stations, airports, and at the central banks. Other areas frequented by foreign shoppers, such as antique stores, sometimes have exchange counters. Some hotels, restaurants, and stores accept foreign currency directly, but generally for the purchase of imported goods only. In the near future, China intends to replace foreign currency with exchange vouchers. Visitors should note the times that the exchange desk is open to avoid disappointment.

Two more points to remember: retain receipts for larger and more expensive purchases and hang on to all the exchange slips which are made out to you after changing money. This will help you with customs and with changing your remaining Chinese currency back to the original or different currency.

| ENGLISH | PINYIN | PRONUNCIATION | CHARACTERS |
|---------|--------|---------------|------------|
| **Money** | qián | chee-en | 钱 |

| ENGLISH | PINYIN | PRONUNCIATION | CHARACTERS |
|---------|--------|---------------|------------|
| **Yuan** | kuài (yuán) | kwhy (yoo-ahn) | 块（元） |
| **Jiao** | máo (jiāo) | mao (jee-ow) | 毛（角） |
| **Fen** | fēn | fun | 分 |
| **One yuan** | yíkuài (qián) | yee–kwhy (chee-en) | 一块（钱） |
| **Two yuan** | liǎngkuài (qián) | lee-ahng–kwhy (chee-en) | 两块（钱） |
| **Five yuan** | wǔkuài (qián) | woo–kwhy (chee-en) | 五块（钱） |
| **Ten yuan** | shíkuài (qián) | shir–kwhy (chee-en) | 十块（钱） |
| **jiao** | yìmáo (qián) | yee–mao (chee-en) | 一毛（钱） |
| **One fen** | yìfēn (qián) | yee–fun (chee-en) | 一分（钱） |
| **Nine fen** | jiǔfēn (qián) | jee-oh–fun (chee-en) | 九分（钱） |
| **Eleven fen** | yìmáo yī | yee–mao yee | 一毛一 |
| **Ninety-five fen** | jiǔmáo wǔ | jee-oh–mao woo | 九毛五 |
| **One yuan fifty-four fen** | yíkuài wǔmáo sì | yee–kwhy woo–mao suh | 一块五毛四 |
| **Chinese people's currency** | rénmínbì | run–meen–bee | 人民币 |
| **Exchange** | duìhuàn | doo-ay–hwahn | 兑换 |

| | | | |
|---|---|---|---|
| **Change money** | huàn qián | hwahn chee-en | 换钱 |
| **Cash a check** | huán zhīpiào | hwahn jir-pee-ow | 换支票 |
| **I would like to change some money.** | Wǒ yào huàn qián. | waw yao hwahn chee-en | 我要换钱 |
| **Where is the exchange?** | Duìhànchù zài nàlǐ/nǎr? | doo-ay-hwahnchoo-dzai nah-lee/nahr | 兑换处在哪里 / 哪儿 |
| **Foreign currency** | wàibì | why-bee | 外币 |
| **American currency / dollars** | měijīn | may-jeen | 美金 |
| **British sterling / pounds** | yīngbàng | ying-bahng | 英镑 |
| **Hong Kong currency / dollars** | gǎngbì | gahng-bee | 港币 |
| **Japanese yen** | rìyuán | rih-yoo-ahn | 日元 |
| **Canadian currency / dollars** | jiābì | jee-ah-bee | 加币 |
| **Australian currency / dollars** | àobì | ow-bee | 澳币 |
| **French francs** | fǎláng | fah-lahng | 法郎 |
| **Swiss francs** | ruìshì fǎláng | ray-shir fah-lahng | 瑞士法郎 |

MONEY

| ENGLISH | PINYIN | PRONUNCIATION | CHARACTERS |
|---|---|---|---|
| Deutsche marks | măkè | mah–kuh | 马克 |
| I have... | Wó yŏu... | waw yo | 我有…… |
| I would like.../ I want... | Wŏ yào... | waw yao | 我要…… |
| Cash (noun) | xiànjīn, xiànkuăn | shee-an–jeen, shee-an–kwahn | 现金，现款 |
| Traveler's check(s) | lŭxíng zhípiào | lü–shing jir–pee-ow | 旅行支票 |
| Bank draft | yínháng zhīpiào | yeen–hahng jir–pee-ow | 银行支票 |
| Letter of credit | xìnyòng zhèngmíng shū | sheen–yoong juhng–ming shoo | 信用证明书 |
| Credit card | xìnyòng kăpiàn | sheen–yoong kah–pee-en | 信用卡片 |
| Letter of introduction | jièshào xìn | jee-yeh–shao sheen | 介绍信 |
| Passport | hùzhào | hoo–jao | 护照 |
| Exchange slip | duìhuàn dān | doo-ay–hwahn dan | 兑换单 |
| I'm sorry. | Duíbŭqĭ. | doo-ay–boo–chee | 对不起…… |
| I didn't bring it. | Wŏ méiyŏu dàilái. | waw may–yo dye–lye | 我没有带来 |
| I've lost it. | Wó bă tā diūlĕ. | waw bah tah dee-oh–luh | 我把它丢了 |

MONEY

| ENGLISH | PINYIN | PRONUNCIATION | CHARACTERS |
|---------|--------|---------------|------------|
| **What should I do?** | Gāi zěnmě bàn? | guy dzum-muh–bahn | 该怎么办？ |
| **This is my signature.** | Zhèi shì wǒdě qiānmíng. | jay shir waw–duh chee-en-ming | 这是我的签名 |
| **No, it's not my signature.** | Bù, búshì wǒdě qiānmíng. | boo, boo–shir waw–duh chee-an-ming | 不，不是我的签名 |
| **Where should I sign?** | Zài nálǐ/nǎr qiān-míng? | dzai nah-lee/nahr chee-an-ming | 在哪里/哪签名？ |
| **Exchange rate** | duìhuàn lù | doo-ay–hwahn lü | 兑换率 |
| **What is the exchange rate today?** | Jīntiāndě duìhuàn lù shì duóshǎo? | jeen–tee-en–duh doo-ay–hwahn lü shir dwaw–shao | 今天的兑换率是多少？ |
| **Please write it down.** | Qíng nǐ xiě xiàlái. | ching nee shee-eh shee-ya lye | 请你写下来 |
| **Notes, bills** | zhǐbì | jir–bee | 纸币 |
| **Small change** | língqián | ling–chee-en | 零钱 |
| **Please give me...** | Qíng géi wǒ... | ching gay waw | 请给我…… |
| **Some bills/notes** | yìxiē zhǐbì | yee-shee-eh jir–bee | 一些纸币 |
| **Some small change** | yìdiǎn língqián | yee-dee-en ling–chee-en | 一点零钱 |

MONEY

| ENGLISH | PINYIN | PRONUNCIATION | CHARACTERS |
|---------|--------|---------------|------------|
| **You gave me too much.** | Ní géi wǒ tài duōlě. | nee gay waw tye dwaw–luh | 你给我太多了 |
| **This is not correct.** | Zhèi búduì. | jay boo–doo-ay | 这不对 |
| **Please count it again.** | Qǐng zài shǔ yìbiàn. | ching dzai shoo yee–bee-en | 请在数一遍 |
| **Please calculate it again.** | Qǐng zài suàn yìbiàn. | ching dzai soo-ahn yee–bee-en | 请在算一遍 |
| **That's correct.** | Duìlě. | doo-ay–luh | 对了 |
| **I'm sorry, my mistake.** | Duìbǔqǐ, wǒ nòng cuòlě. | doo-ay–boo–chee, waw noong tswaw–luh | 对不起, 我弄错了 |
| **It's nothing. Don't worry about it.** | Méiguānxǐ. Bú yàojǐn. | may–gwan–shee. boo yao–jeen | 没关系。 不要紧 |
| **Thank you.** | Xièxiě. | shee-eh shee-eh. | 谢谢 |
| **When do you open?** | Shénmě shíhòu kāi mén? | shummah shir–hoe kye mun | 什么时候开门？ |
| **When do you close?** | Shénmě shíhòu guān mén? | shummah shir–hoe gwan mun | 什么时候关门？ |

| ENGLISH | PINYIN | PRONUNCIATION | CHARACTERS |
|---------|--------|---------------|------------|
| **Wallet** | pí jiāzǐ | pee jee-ah–dzih | 皮夹子 |
| **Purse** | qiánbāo | chee-an–bao | 钱包 |
| **Safe/safety deposit** | báoxiǎnxiāng | bao–shee-en shee-ahng | 保险箱 |
| **Bank** | yínháng | yeen–hung | 银行 |
| **Central bank** | zǒngháng | dzoong–hung | 总行 |
| **Where is...** | ...zài nálǐ/nǎr? | ...dzai nah–lee/nahr | ...在哪里/哪儿？ |

# WEATHER

| ENGLISH | PINYIN | PRONUNCIATION | CHARACTERS |
|---|---|---|---|
| **Weather** | tiānquǐ | tee-en-chee | 天气 |
| **Today's weather is...** | Jīntiāndé tiānqi... | jeen-tee-en-duh tee-en-chee | 今天的 天气…… |
| **Good** | hǎo | hao | 好 |
| **Not good** | bù hǎo | boo hao | 不好 |
| **Cold** | lěng | lung | 冷 |
| **Hot** | rè | ruh | 热 |
| **Cool** | liáng | lee-ahng | 凉 |
| **Warm** | nuǎn | noo-ahn | 暖 |
| **Humid, sultry** | mēn | mun | 闷 |
| **Damp, wet** | cháoshī | chao-shir | 潮湿 |
| **Dry** | gānzào | gahn-dzao | 干燥 |
| **Wind** | fēng | fung | 风 |
| **Rain** | yǔ | yü | 雨 |
| **Cloud** | yún | yoo-win | 云 |
| **Sun** | taìyǎng | tye-yahng | 太阳 |

| ENGLISH | PINYIN | PRONUNCIATION | CHARACTERS |
|---------|--------|---------------|------------|
| **Snow** | xuě | shoo-eh | 雪 |
| **Fog** | wù | woo | 雾 |
| **Ice** | bīng | bing | 冰 |
| **It's windy.** | Guā fēnglě | gwah fung–luh | 刮风了 |
| **It's raining.** | Xià yǔlě | shee-ya yü–luh | 下雨了 |
| **It's cloudy, dull.** | Shìyīntiān. | shir yeen–tee-en | 是阴天 |
| **It's snowing.** | Xià xuělě. | shee-ya shoo-eh–luh | 下雪了 |
| **It's sunny.** | Taìyáng chūláile. | tye–yahng choo–lye–luh | 太阳出来了 |
| **It's a clear day.** | Shì qíngtiān. | shir ching–tee-en | 是 晴天 |
| **Thunder** | léi | lay | 雷 |
| **Lightning** | shāndiàn | shahn–dee-en | 闪电 |
| **Storm** | bàofēngyǔ | bao–fung–yü | 暴风雨 |
| **Thunderstorm** | léiyǔ | lay–yü | 雷雨 |
| **Sandstorm** | dà fēngshā | dah fung–shah | 大风沙 |
| **Heavy rain** | dà yǔ | da yü | 大雨 |
| **Typhoon** | táifēng | tye–fung | 台风 |
| **Gale** | kuángfēng | kwahng–fung | 狂风 |

| ENGLISH | PINYIN | PRONUNCIATION | CHARACTERS |
|---|---|---|---|
| **Cold front** | hánliú | han–lee-oh | 寒流 |
| **What a nice day!** | Tiānqǐ zhēn hǎo! | teen-en–chee juhn hao | 天气真好！ |
| **What a lousy day!** | Tiānqǐ zhēn zāo! | tee-en–chee juhn dzao | 天气真糟！ |
| **Temperature** | wēndù | win–doo | 温度 |
| **What is the temperature today?** | Jīntiānde wēndù shì shénme? | jeen-tee-en–duh win–doo shir shummah | 今天温度是什么？ |
| **Thermometer** | wēndù biǎo | win–doo bee-ow | 温度表 |
| **Barometer** | qìyā biǎo | chee-ya bee-ow | 气压表 |
| **Forecast** | tiānqǐ yùbào | tee-en–chee yü–bao | 天气预报 |
| **What is the forecast for tomorrow?** | Míngtiānde tiānqǐ yùbào shì shénme? | ming–tee-en–duh tee-en–chee yü–bao shir shummah | 明天的天气预报是什么？ |

Hotel accommodations for most travelers are pre-arranged by China International Travel Service. Rates and facilities vary from city to city, but most hotels that serve foreigners have similar amenities. Rooms are simple and functional. They usually contain twin beds, a desk, an easy chair, a bureau, and a bathroom. Hot and cold drinking water is provided. Lighting is often inadequate for reading purposes.

Most hotels have postal, banking, telegraph, and cable facilities on the premises. Shops sell snacks, travel items, and handicrafts. Room service is available, as are laundry and telephone services.

Generally speaking, most tour groups and visiting delegations take all of their meals at the hotel. Meals are served at predesignated times at pre-assigned tables. A choice of Western or Chinese dishes is usually available in the major cities providing that requests are made early enough.

| *ENGLISH* | *PINYIN* | *PRONUNCIATION* | *CHARACTERS* |
|---|---|---|---|
| **Hotel** | fàndiàn, bīnguǎn lúguǎn | fan–dee-en, been–gwan lü–gwan | 饭店，宾馆，旅馆 |
| **Room** | fángjiān | fahng–jee-en | 房间 |
| **Empty room** | kōng fángjiān | koong fahng–jee-en | 空房间 |
| **Single room** | dānrén fángjiān | dan–run fahng–jee-en | 单人房间 |
| **Double room** | shuāngrén fángjiān | shoo-ahng–run fahng–jee-en | 双人房间 |

| ENGLISH | PINYIN | PRONUNCIATION | CHARACTERS |
|---------|--------|---------------|------------|
| **Suite** | tàofáng | tao-fahng | 套房 |
| **Do you have a…?** | Yŏu méiyŏu…? | yo may-yo | 有没有…? |
| **I'd like a…** | Wŏ yào yígè… | waw yao yee-guh | 我要一个… |
| **I'd like to reserve a…** | Wŏ yào dìng yígè… | waw yao ding yee-guh | 我要定一个… |
| **How much is it?** | Duóshăo qián? | dwaw-shao chee-en | 多少钱? |
| **Lobby** | qiántīng | chee-en-ting | 前厅 |
| **Elevator** | diàntī | dee-en-tee | 电梯 |
| **Stairs** | lóutī | low-tee | 楼梯 |
| **Ground floor** | dĭlóu | dee-low | 底楼 |
| **Top floor** | dĭnglóu | ding-low | 顶楼 |
| **Going up** | shàng | shahng | 上 |
| **Going down** | xià | shee-ya | 下 |
| **Registration** | dēngjìtái | dung-jee-tye | 登记台 |
| **Register** | dēngjì | dung-jee | 登记 |
| **Reservation** | yùdìng fángjiān | yü-ding fahng-jee-en | 预定房间 |
| **Passport** | hùzhào | hoo-jao | 护照 |

| ENGLISH | PINYIN | PRONUNCIATION | CHARACTERS |
|---------|--------|---------------|------------|
| **Visa** | qiānzhèng | chee-en–juhng | 签证 |
| **Luggage** | xínglǐ | shing–lee | 行李 |
| **Room number** | fánghào | fahng–hao | 房号 |
| **Key** | yàoshǐ | yao–shir | 钥匙 |
| **Door** | mén | mun | 门 |
| **Bed** | chuáng | chwahng | 床 |
| **Quilt** | bèizǐ | bay–dzih | 被子 |
| **Sheets** | chuángdān | chwahng–dan | 床单 |
| **Pillow** | zhěntóu | juhn-toe | 枕头 |
| **Bath** | xízǎogāng | shee–dzao–gahng | 洗澡缸 |
| **Towel** | máojīn | mao–jeen | 毛巾 |
| **Soap** | féizào | fay–dzao | 肥皂 |
| **Toilet** | cèsuǒ | tse–swo | 厕所 |
| **Toilet paper** | wèishēngzhǐ | way–shahng jir | 卫生纸 |
| **Faucet** | lóngtóu | loong–toe | 龙头 |
| **Plug** | sāizǐ | sye–dzih | 塞子 |
| **Water** | shuǐ | shway | 水 |

| ENGLISH | PINYIN | PRONUNCIATION | CHARACTERS |
|---------|--------|---------------|------------|
| **Window** | chuánghǔ | chwahng–hoo | 窗户 |
| **Curtains** | chuánglián | chwahng–lee-en | 窗帘 |
| **Mirror** | jìngzǐ | jing–dzih | 镜子 |
| **Carpet** | dìtǎn | dee–tan | 地毯 |
| **Electric light** | diàndēng | dee-en–dung | 电灯 |
| **Light bulb** | dēngpào | dung–pao | 灯泡 |
| | | | |
| **Turn the light on.** | Kāi dēng. | kye–dung | 开灯 |
| **Turn the light off.** | Guān dēng. | gwan–dung | 关灯 |
| | | | |
| **Radio** | shōuyīnjī | show–yeen–jee | 收音机 |
| **Television** | diànshìjī | dee-an–shir–jee | 电视机 |
| **Air conditioning** | lěngqì | lung–chee | 冷气 |
| **Heating** | nuǎnqì | noo-ahn–chee | 暖气 |
| **Electric fan** | diànshàn | dee-en–shan | 电扇 |
| **Telephone** | diànhuà | dee-en–hwa | 电话 |
| **Long-distance call** | chángtú diànhuà | chahng–too dee-en–hwa | 长途电话 |
| | | | |
| **It's dirty.** | Zāngle. | dzahng–luh | 脏了 |

| ENGLISH | PINYIN | PRONUNCIATION | CHARACTERS |
|---|---|---|---|
| **It's broken.** | Huàilě. | hwhy–luh | 坏了 |
| **Sleep** | shuìjiào | shway–jee-ow | 睡觉 |
| **Get up** | qǐchuáng | chee–chwahng | 起床 |
| **Alarm clock** | nàozhōng | nao–joong | 闹钟 |
| **Knock on the door** | qiāomén | chee-ow–mun | 敲门 |
| **Call** | jiào | jee-ow | 叫 |
| **We don't have...** | Wǒmen méiyǒu... | waw–mun may–yo | 我们没有… |
| **Thermos** | nuánshuǐ píng | noo-ahn shway–ping | 暖水瓶 |
| **Glasses** | bēizǐ | bay–dzih | 杯子 |
| **Drinking water** | yīngyòng shuǐ | yeen–yoong shway | 饮用水 |
| **Ashtray** | yānhuīgāng | yen–hway gang | 烟灰缸 |
| **Ink** | mòshuǐ | moh–shway | 墨水 |
| **Letter paper** | xìnzhǐ | sheen-jir | 信纸 |
| **Envelope** | xìnfēng | sheen–fung | 信封 |
| **Hanger** | guàyījià | gwah–yee-jee-ah | 挂衣架 |
| | | | |
| **Laundry** | xǐyīdiàn | shee–yee–dee-en | 洗染店 |
| **Dry clean** | gānxǐ | gahn–shee | 干洗 |
| **When will it be ready?** | Shénme shíhòu néng xǐ hǎo? | shummah shir–hoe nung shee–hao | 什么时候能 洗好？ |

| ENGLISH | PINYIN | PRONUNCIATION | CHARACTERS |
|---------|--------|---------------|------------|
| **I'm leaving tomorrow.** | Wǒ míngtiān zǒu. | waw ming–tee-en dzou | 我明天走 |
| **I'm leaving the day after tomorrow.** | Wǒ hòutiān zǒu. | waw hoe–tee-en dzou | 我后天走 |
| **Where is the...?** | ...zài nálǐ/nǎr | dzai nah–lee/nahr | ...在哪里/哪儿？ |
| **Exchange** | duìhuàn | doo-ay hwahn | 对换 |
| **Post office** | yóujú | yo–jü | 邮局 |
| **Barber shop (hotel)** | lǐfà shì | lee–fah shir | 理发室 |
| **Cafe** | kāfēi diàn | kay–fay dee-an | 咖啡店 |
| **Restroom** | cèsuǒ | tse–swo | 厕所 |
| **Dining room** | cāntīng | tsahn–ting | 餐厅 |
| **Shop** | xiǎo màibù | shee-ow my–boo | 小卖部 |
| **Information desk** | fúwùchù | foo–woo–choo | 服务处 |
| **Telegram** | diànbào | dee-en bao | 电报 |
| **Air letter** | hángkōng yóujiàn | hahng–koong yo–jee-an | 航空邮件 |
| **Postcard** | míngxìngpiàn | ming–sheen–pee-en | 明信片 |
| **Stamps** | yóupiào | yo–pee-ow | 邮票 |

| ENGLISH | PINYIN | PRONUNCIATION | CHARACTERS |
|---------|--------|---------------|-----------|
| **What is the name of this hotel?** | Zhèigě fàndiàn jiào shénmě míngzǐ? | jay–guh fan–dee-en jee-ow shummah ming–dzih | 这个饭店叫 什么名子？ |
| **Where is the Friend-ship Store?** | Yǒuyì Shāngdiàn zài nálǐ/nǎr? | yo–yee shahng–dee-en dzai nah–lee/nahr | 友谊商店在 哪里／哪儿？ |
| **Is it far to walk?** | Zǒu lù yuǎn bù yuǎn? | dzou–loo yoo-ahn-boo–yoo-ahn | 走路远不远？ |
| **I would like to call a taxi.** | Wǒ yào yígè chūzūqìchē. | waw yao yee–guh choo–dzoo–chee-cheh | 我要一个出 租汽车 |
| **I would like to go to...** | Wǒ yào qù... | waw yao chü | 我要去…… |
| **Where is the tour bus?** | Wǒměndě chē zài nálǐ? | waw–mun–duh cheh dzai nah–lee | 我们的车在 哪里？ |
| **Please come in.** | Qǐng jìn. | ching jeen | 请进 |
| **Please sit down.** | Qǐng zuò. | ching dzwaw | 请坐 |
| **Please wait a minute.** | Qíng nǐ děngyìděng. | ching nee dung–yee–dung | 请你等一等 |
| **Where can I buy a map?** | Wó nálǐ/nǎr kéyǐ mǎi yígè dìtú? | waw nah–lee/nahr kuh–yee my yee–guh dee–too | 我哪里／ 哪儿可以买 一个地图？ |

HOTELS

| ENGLISH | PINYIN | PRONUNCIATION | CHARACTERS |
| --- | --- | --- | --- |
| **Where are we?** | Wǒmen zài nálǐ/nǎr? | waw–mun dzai nah–lee/nahr | 我们在哪里/哪儿? |
| **Has anyone come to look for me?** | Yǒu méiyǒu rén lái zháo wǒ? | yo may–yo run lai jao waw | 有没有人来找我? |

| ENGLISH | PINYIN | PRONUNCIATION | CHARACTERS |
|---|---|---|---|
| **I'm hungry.** | Wǒ è'lě. | waw uh–luh | 我饿了 |
| **I'm famished.** | Wǒ è jílě. | waw uh–jee–luh | 我饿极了 |
| **I'm not hungry.** | Wǒ bú è. | waw boo–uh | 我不饿 |
| **I've eaten.** | Wǒ yǐjīng chīlě. | waw yee–jing chir–luh | 我已经吃了 |
| **I'm full.** | Wǒ chī bǎolě. | waw chir bao–luh | 我吃饱了 |
| **No more, thanks.** | Gòulě, xièxiě. | go–luh, shee–eh–shee–eh | 够了, 谢谢 |
| | | | |
| **Dining room** | cāntīng | tsahn–ting | 餐厅 |
| **Restaurant** | fànguǎn | fan–gwan | 饭馆 |
| | | | |
| **When does it open?** | Shénmě shíhòu kāi mén? | shummah shir–hoe kye–mun | 什么时候开门？ |
| **When does it close?** | Shénmě shíhòu guān mén? | shummah shir–hoe gwan–mun | 什么时候关门？ |
| | | | |
| **We are the...group.** | Wǒmen shì... tuándě. | waw–mun shir... twahn–duh | 我们是……团的 |
| **American** | Měiguó | may–gwaw | 美国 |

| ENGLISH | PINYIN | PRONUNCIATION | CHARACTERS |
|---|---|---|---|
| **Canadian** | Jiānádà | jee-ah–nah–dah | 加拿大 |
| **English** | Yīngguó | ying–gwaw | 英国 |
| **Australian** | Àodàlìyà | ow–dah–lee–yah | 澳大利亚 |
| **New Zealand** | Xīnxīlán | sheen–shee–lahn | 新西兰 |
| **French** | Fǎguó | Fah–gwaw | 法国 |
| **German** | Déguó | duh–gwaw | 德国 |
| **Japanese** | Rìběn | rih–bun | 日本 |
| **Italian** | Yìdàlì | yee–dah–lee | 意大利 |
| | | | |
| **Where do we sit?** | Gāi zuò zài nǎr? | guy dzwaw dzai nahr | 该坐在哪儿？ |
| **There are...of us.** | Wǒmén yígòng... rén. | waw–mun yee–goong ...run | 我们一共… …人 |
| **Two** | liǎnggě | lee-ahng–guh | 两个 |
| **Three** | sāngě | san–guh | 三个 |
| **Four** | sìgě | suh–guh | 四个 |
| **Five** | wǔgě | woo–guh | 五个 |
| **Six** | liùgě | lee-oh–guh | 六个 |
| **Seven** | qīgě | chee–guh | 七个 |
| **Eight** | bāgě | bah–guh | 八个 |
| **Nine** | jiǔgě | jee-oh–guh | 九个 |

| ENGLISH | PINYIN | PRONUNCIATION | CHARACTERS |
|---------|--------|---------------|------------|
| **Ten** | shígě | shir–guh | 十个 |
| **There's only me.** | Zhí wǒ yígè. | jir waw yee–guh | 只我一个 |
| **We'd like to eat...** | Wǒmen yào chī... | waw–mun yao chir | 我们要吃… |
| **Western food** | xīcān | shee–tsahn | 西餐 |
| **Chinese food** | zhōngcān | joong–tsahn | 中餐 |
| **We'd like to see a menu.** | Wǒmen yào kàn-kǎn càidān. | waw–mun yao kahn–kahn tseye–daw | 我们要看看菜单 |
| **Breakfast** | zǎofàn | dzao–fan | 早饭 |
| **Lunch** | wūfàn | woo–fan | 午饭 |
| **Dinner** | wǎnfàn | wahn–fan | 晚饭 |
| **I don't have...** | Wǒ méiyǒu... | waw may–yo | 我没有 |
| **Chopsticks** | kuàizǐ | kwhy–dzih | 筷子 |
| **Fork** | chā | cha | 叉 |
| **Knife** | dāo | dao | 刀 |
| **Spoon** | sháo | shao | 勺 |
| **Cup** | bēi | bay | 杯 |

**FOOD & DRINK**

| ENGLISH | PINYIN | PRONUNCIATION | CHARACTERS |
|---|---|---|---|
| **Teacup** | chábēi | cha–bay | 茶杯 |
| **Glass** | bólí bēi | baw–lee bay | 玻璃杯 |
| **Plate** | pánzǐ | pan–dzih | 盘子 |
| **Bowl** | wǎn | wahn | 碗 |
| **Napkin** | cānjīn | tsahn–jeen | 餐巾 |
| **Toothpicks** | yáqiān | yah–chee-en | 牙签 |
| | | | |
| **I'd like to drink...** | Wǒ yào hē... | waw yao huh | 我要喝…… |
| **Beer** | píjiǔ | pee–jee-oh | 啤酒 |
| **Hot water** | kāishuǐ | kye–shway | 开水 |
| **Cold water** | lěng kāishuǐ | lung kye–shway | 冷开水 |
| **Mineral water** | kuàngquán shuǐ | kwahng chwan shway | 矿泉水 |
| **Soft drink** | qìshuǐ | chee–shway | 汽水 |
| **Tea** | chá | cha | 茶 |
| **Chinese tea** | lǜchá | lü–cha | 绿茶 |
| **Western tea** | hóngchá | hoong–cha | 红茶 |
| **Coffee** | kāfēi | kah–fay | 咖啡 |
| **Milk** | niúnǎi | nee-oh–nye | 牛奶 |
| **Juice** | shuíguǒ zhī | shway–gwaw jir | 水果汁 |

| ENGLISH | PINYIN | PRONUNCIATION | CHARACTERS |
|---|---|---|---|
| **Wine** | jiǔ, pútǎo jiǔ | jee-oh, poo-tao jee-oh | 酒，葡萄酒 |
| **Cold** | lěng | lung | 冷 |
| **Do you have it cold?** | Yǒu méiyǒu lěngdě? | yo may-yo lung-duh | 有没有冷的？ |
| **Fresh** | xīnxiāndě | sheen-shee-en-duh | 新鲜的 |
| **Canned** | guàntóudě | gwan-toe-duh | 罐头的 |
| **Rice** | mǐfàn | mee-fan | 米饭 |
| **Bread** | miànbāo | mee-en-bao | 面包 |
| **Noodles** | miàntiáo | mee-en-tee-ow | 面条 |
| **Steamed buns** | mántǒu | man-toe | 馒头 |
| **Steamed rolls** | huā juǎr | hwa-jwar | 花卷 |
| **Potatoes** | tǔdòu | too-doe | 土豆 |
| **Eggs** | jīdàn | jee-dan | 鸡蛋 |
| **Fried eggs** | jiān jīdàn | jee-en jee-dan | 煎鸡蛋 |
| **Scrambled eggs** | chǎo jīdàn | chao jee-dan | 炒鸡蛋 |
| **Boiled eggs** | zhǔ jīdàn | jew jee-dan | 煮鸡蛋 |
| **Meat** | ròu | row | 肉 |

**FOOD & DRINK**

| ENGLISH | PINYIN | PRONUNCIATION | CHARACTERS |
|---|---|---|---|
| **Beef** | niúròu | nee-oh-row | 牛肉 |
| **Pork** | zhūròu | jew-row | 猪肉 |
| **Mutton** | yángròu | yahng-row | 羊肉 |
| **Chicken** | jī | jee | 鸡 |
| **Duck** | yā | yah | 鸭 |
| **Fish** | yú | yü | 鱼 |
| **Sturgeon, doré** | huángyú | hwahng-yü | 黄鱼 |
| **Carp** | lǐyú | lee-yü | 鲤鱼 |
| **Mackerel** | qīngyú | ching-yü | 鲭鱼 |
| **Eel** | mànyú | man-yü | 鳗鱼 |
| **Cuttle fish** | yóuyú | yo-yü | 鱿鱼 |
| **Shrimp** | xiā | shee-ya | 虾 |
| **Prawn** | dà xiā | dah shee-ya | 大虾 |
| **Crab** | pángxiè | pahng-shee-ya | 螃蟹 |
| **Boil, cook** | zhǔ | jew | 煮 |
| **Fry** | jiān | jee-en | 煎 |
| **Stir-fry** | chǎo | chao | 炒 |

| ENGLISH | PINYIN | PRONUNCIATION | CHARACTERS |
|---|---|---|---|
| **Steam** | zhēng | juhng | 蒸 |
| **Roast** | kǎo | kao | 烤 |
| **Cook in a red sauce** | hóngshāo | hoong–shao | 红烧 |
| **Ginger** | jiāng | jee-ahng | 姜 |
| **Chili pepper** | làjiāo | lah–jee-ow | 辣椒 |
| **Garlic** | suàn | soo-ahn | 蒜 |
| **Oil** | yóu | yo | 油 |
| **Salt** | yán | yen | 盐 |
| **Pepper** | hújiāo fěn | hoo–jee-ow fun | 胡椒粉 |
| **Sugar** | táng | tahng | 糖 |
| **Vinegar** | cù | tsoo | 醋 |
| **Soy sauce** | jiàngyóu | jee-ahng–yo | 酱油 |
| **Butter** | huángyóu | hwahng–yo | 黄油 |
| **Ketchup** | fānqié zhī | fan–chyeh jir | 番茄汁 |
| **Soup** | tāng | tahng | 汤 |
| **Vegetables** | shūcài | shoo–tsai | 蔬菜 |
| **White cabbage** | báicài | bye–tseye | 白菜 |

| ENGLISH | PINYIN | PRONUNCIATION | CHARACTERS |
|---|---|---|---|
| **Tomato** | xīhóngshì | shee–hoong–shir | 西红柿 |
| **Eggplant** | qiézǐ | chyeh–dzih | 茄子 |
| **Turnip** | luóbǒ | lwaw–baw | 萝卜 |
| **Cucumber** | huángguā | hwahng–gwah | 黄瓜 |
| **Green onions** | cōng | tsoong | 葱 |
| **Mushroom** | mógǔ | moh–goo | 蘑菇 |
| **Spinach** | bōcài | baw–tseye | 菠菜 |
| **String beans** | biǎndòu | bee-en-doe | 扁豆 |
| **Bamboo shoots** | sūn | swun | 笋 |
| **Bean sprouts** | dòuyá | doe–yah | 豆芽 |
| **Lotus root** | ǒu | oh | 藕 |
| **Carrots** | hóng luóbǒ | hoong lwaw–baw | 红萝卜 |
| **Corn** | yù mǐ | yü–mee | 玉米 |
| **Salad** | shālā | shah–lah | 沙拉 |
| **Bean curd** | dòufū | doe–foo | 豆腐 |
| **Fruit** | shuíguǒ | shway–gwaw | 水果 |
| **Apple** | píngguǒ | ping–gwaw | 苹果 |
| **Orange** | júzǐ | jü–dzih | 橘子 |

| ENGLISH | PINYIN | PRONUNCIATION | CHARACTERS |
|---------|--------|---------------|------------|
| **Chinese pear** | lízǐ | lee–dzih | 梨子 |
| **Lichee** | lìzhī | lee–jir | 荔枝 |
| **Persimmon** | shìzǐ | shir–dzih | 柿子 |
| **Lemon** | níngméng | ning–mung | 柠檬 |
| **Peach** | táozǐ | tao–dzih | 桃子 |
| **Sweet melon** | tián guā | tee-en–gwah | 甜瓜 |
| **Watermelon** | xī guā | shee–gwah | 西瓜 |
| **Pineapple** | bōluó | baw–lwaw | 菠萝 |
| **Banana** | xiāngjiāo | shee-ahng–jee-ow | 香蕉 |
| **Plum** | lǐzǐ | lee–dzih | 李子 |
| **Dessert** | tiánpǐn | tee-en–peen | 甜品 |
| **Candied apple** | bāsī píngguǒ | bah–suh ping–gwaw | 拔丝苹果 |
| **Ice cream** | bīngqīlín | bing–chee–leen | 冰淇淋 |
| **Almond bean curd** | xìngrén dòufǔ | shing–run doe–foo | 杏仁豆腐 |
| **Apple pie** | píngguǒ pái | ping–gwaw pie | 苹果排 |
| **Cake** | dàngāo | dan–gao | 蛋糕 |
| **Dumpling** | jiǎozǐ | jee-ow–dzih | 饺子 |
| **Boiled dumpling** | shuǐjiǎo | shway–jee-ow | 水饺 |
| **Steamed dumpling** | zhēngjiǎo | juhng–jee-ow | 蒸饺 |

| ENGLISH | PINYIN | PRONUNCIATION | CHARACTERS |
|---|---|---|---|
| **Fried dumpling** | guōtiē | gwaw–tee-eh | 锅贴 |
| **Steamed buns** | bāozǐ | bao–dzih | 包子 |
| **Peanuts** | huāshēng | hwa–shung | 花生 |
| **Chocolate** | qiǎokèlì | chee-ow–kuh–lee | 巧克力 |
| **Candy** | táng | tahng | 糖 |
| **Chewing gum** | kǒuxiāngtáng | kou shee-ahng–tahng | 口香糖 |
| **Biscuits/cookies** | bǐnggān | bing–gahn | 饼干 |
| **Toast** | kǎo miànbāo | kao mee-en–bao | 烤面包 |
| **Jam** | guǒjiàng | gwaw–jee-ahng | 果酱 |
| **Yogurt** | suān niúnǎi | soo-ahn nee-oh–nye | 酸牛奶 |
| **Juice** | shuíguǒ zhī | shway–gwaw jir | 水果汁 |
| **Ham** | huótuǐ | hwa–too-ay | 火腿 |
| **Porridge** | zhōu | joe | 粥 |
| **Salted vegetables** | xián cài | shee-en–tsai | 咸菜 |
| **Noodles in soup** | tāngmiàn | tahng–mee-en | 汤面 |
| **Won ton** | húntǔn | hwoon–dwin | 馄饨 |
| **Dim sum** | diǎnxīn | dee-en–sheen | 点心 |

| ENGLISH | PINYIN | PRONUNCIATION | CHARACTERS |
|---|---|---|---|
| **Maotai** | máotái | mao–tye | 茅台 |
| **Brandy** | báilándì | bye–lahn–dee | 白兰地 |
| **Chinese liquor** | báijiŭ | bye–jee-oh | 白酒 |
| **Beer** | píjiŭ | pee–jee-oh | 啤酒 |
| **Wine** | pútǎo jiŭ | poo–tao–jee-oh | 葡萄酒 |
| **Bottoms up/cheers!** | Gānbēi! | gahn–bay | 干杯 |
| **I didn't order this.** | Zhèi búshì wó diǎndě. | jay boo–shir waw dee-en–duh | 这不是我点的 |
| **I ordered…** | Wó diǎndě shì… | waw dee-en–duh shir | 我点的是… |
| **This is too…** | Zhèi tài…lě | jay tye…luh | 这太……了 |
| **Hot (spicy)** | là | lah | 辣 |
| **Salty** | xián | shee-en | 咸 |
| **Sweet** | tián | tee-en | 甜 |
| **Sour** | suān | soo-ahn | 酸 |
| **Bland** | dàn | dan | 淡 |
| **This food is cold.** | Zhèi cài shì lěngdě. | jay tseye shir lung–duh | 这菜是冷的 |
| **Waiter/waitress** | fúwùyuán | foo–woo–yoo-ahn | 服务员 |
| **We've been waiting for a long time.** | Wǒmén děnglě bàntiānlě. | waw–mun dung–luh bahn–tee-en–luh | 我们等了半天了 |

**FOOD & DRINK**

| ENGLISH | PINYIN | PRONUNCIATION | CHARACTERS |
|---|---|---|---|
| **The food was good.** | Hén hǎo chī. | hun hao chir | 很好吃 |
| **Could I have the bill, please.** | Qíng nǐ suàn zhàng. | ching nee soo-ahn jahng | 请你算账 |
| **What was the name of that dish?** | Nèige cài jiào shénmě? | nay–guh tseye jee-ow shummah | 那个菜叫什么？ |
| **Please write that down.** | Qíng nǐ xiěxiàlái. | ching nee shee-eh shee-ya-lye | 请你写下来 |
| **Thank you.** | Xièxiě. | shee-eh–shee-eh | 谢谢 |

| ENGLISH | PINYIN | PRONUNCIATION | CHARACTERS |
|---------|--------|---------------|------------|

## AT THE POST OFFICE

| ENGLISH | PINYIN | PRONUNCIATION | CHARACTERS |
|---------|--------|---------------|------------|
| Post office | yóujú | yo–jü | 邮局 |
| Stamps | yóupiào | yo–pee-ow | 邮票 |
| To send to… | jì dào…qù | jee dao…chü | 寄到……去 |
| Air mail | hángkōng | hahng–koong | 航空 |
| Surface mail | píngyóu | ping–yo | 平邮 |
| Express | tèkuài | tuh–kwhy | 特快 |
| Registered | guàhào | gwah–hao | 挂号 |
| Glue | jiāoshuǐ | jee-ow–shway | 胶水 |
| Air letter | hángkōng yóujiàn | hahng–koong yo–jee-an | 航空邮件 |
| Postcard | míngxìnpiàn | ming–sheen–pee-en | 明信片 |
| A letter | yì fēngxìn | yee fung sheen | 一封信 |
| Box | hé | huh | 盒 |
| String | shéngzǐ | shung–dzih | 绳子 |
| Binding tape | zādài | dzah–dye | 扎带 |

| ENGLISH | PINYIN | PRONUNCIATION | CHARACTERS |
|---------|--------|---------------|------------|
| **Where can I buy...** | Wó năr kéyĭ măi... | waw nahr kuh-yee my | 我哪儿可以买·· |
| **How much is it?** | Duóshăo qián? | dwaw-shao chee-en | 多少钱？ |
| **How long will it take?** | Huì yào duócháng shíjiān? | hway yao dwaw-chahng shir-jee-en | 会要多长时间？ |
| **When does it open/ close?** | Shénmĕ shíhòu kāi/guān mén? | shummah shir-hoe kye/gwan-mun | 什么时候开/ 关门 |

## AT THE TELEGRAPH OFFICE

| | | | |
|---------|--------|---------------|------------|
| **Telegraph office** | diànbàojú | dee-en-bao jü | 电报局 |
| **Send a telegram** | fā diànbào | fah dee-en-bao | 发电局 |
| **Telegraph form** | diànbàodān | dee-en-bao dan | 电报单 |
| **To...(destination)** | dào... | dao | 到…… |
| **When will it be received?** | Shénmĕ shíhòu kéyĭ shōu dáo? | shummah shir-hoe kuh-yee show-dao | 什么时候可 以收到？ |
| **How much is it per word?** | Mĕi yígè cí duó-shăo qián? | may yee-guh tsih dwaw-shao chee-en | 每一个词多 少钱？ |

## ON THE TELEPHONE

| | | | |
|---------|--------|---------------|------------|
| **Telephone** | diànhuà | dee-en-hwa | 电话 |

| ENGLISH | PINYIN | PRONUNCIATION | CHARACTERS |
|---------|--------|---------------|------------|
| **To telephone, make a call** | dǎ diànhuà | dah dee-en–hwa | 打电话 |
| **Dial** | bō | baw | 拨 |
| **Telephone number** | diànhuà hàomǎ | dee-en–hwa hao-mah | 电话号码 |
| **What is the number of...?** | ...dě diànhuà hàomǎ shì shénmě | ...duh dee-en–hwa hao-mah shir shummah | ...的电话号码是什么? |
| **Please write it down.** | Qǐng nǐ xiěxiàlái. | ching nee shee-eh shee-ya lye | 请你写下来 |
| **I can't get through.** | Wó dǎ bùtōng. | waw dah boo–toong | 我打不通 |
| **The line is busy.** | Zhàn xiàn lě. | jahn shee-en–luh | 占线了 |
| **It's broken.** | Huàilě. | hwhy–luh | 坏了 |
| **Hello?** | Wéi? | way | 喂? |
| **I'm looking for...** | Wó zhǎo... | waw jao | 我找……? |
| **Who are you looking for?** | Ní zhǎo shéi? | nee jao shway | 你找谁 |
| **Who are you?** | Ní nǎlǐ? | nee nah–lee | 你哪里? |
| **I'm sorry, I don't understand.** | Duìbǔqǐ, wǒ tīng bùdǒng. | doo-ay–boo–chee, waw ting boo–doong | 对不起, 我听不懂 |
| **Wait a minute.** | Děng yíxià. | dung yee–shee-ya | 等一下 |
| **Please speak slowly.** | Qǐng màn yìdiǎr. | ching man yee– dee-are | 请慢一点 |

| ENGLISH | PINYIN | PRONUNCIATION | CHARACTERS |
|---------|--------|---------------|------------|
| **Please speak louder.** | Qǐng dàshēng yìdiǎr. | ching dah–shung yee–dee–are | 请大声一点 |
| **You have the wrong number.** | Nǐ dǎ cuòle. | nee dah tswaw–luh | 你打错了 |
| **Hang up the phone.** | Guà diànhuà. | gwah dee-an hwa | 挂电话 |
| **Long-distance call** | chángtú diànhuà | chahng–too dee-en–hwa | 长途电话 |
| **To make a long-distance call** | dǎ chángtú diànhuà | dah chahng–too dee-en–hwa | 打长途电话 |
| **Please give me extension...** | Qǐng zhuǎn.... | ching jew-ahn | 请转 |
| **He/she isn't here/there.** | Tā bú zài./Tā méi zài. | tah boo–dzai/tah may–dzai | 他(她)不在/他(她)没在 |
| **No one is answering.** | Méi rén jiē diànhuà. | may run jee-yeh dee-en–hwa | 没人接电话 |
| **My telephone number is...** | Wǒde diànhuà hàomǎ shì... | waw–duh dee-en–hwa hao–mah shir | 我的电话号码是…… |
| **Do you speak English?** | Nǐ huì shuō Yīngwén mǎ? | nee hway shwaw ying–win mah | 你会说英文吗？ |

| ENGLISH | PINYIN | PRONUNCIATION | CHARACTERS |
|---|---|---|---|
| **Do you like...?** | Ní xǐhuān...mǎ? | nee shee–hwan...mah | 你喜欢⋯ ⋯吗? |
| **I'd like to see...** | Wó xiǎng kàn... | waw shee-ahng kahn | 我想看⋯ |
| **Action (as in fun)** | rènào | ruh–nao | 热闹 |
| **Ticket** | piào | pee-ow | 票 |
| **Where's my seat?** | Wǒdě zuòwèi zài nálǐ/nǎr? | waw–duh dzwaw–way dzai nah–lee/nahr | 我的座位在 哪里/哪儿? |
| **When does (the show) begin?** | Shénmě shíhòu kāishǐ? | shummah shir–hoe kai–shir | 什么时候开 始? |
| **When does (the show) finish?** | Shénmě shíhòu jiéshù | shummah shir–hoe jee–yeh–shoo | 什么时候结 束? |
| **It's too slow moving.** | Tài màn. | tye man | 太慢 |
| **What a bore** | zhēn wúliáo/zhēn méi yìsi | juhn woo–lee–ow/juhn may–yee–suh | 真无聊/ 真没意思 |
| **I'd like to go.** | Wǒ yào zǒu. | waw yao dzou | 我要走 |
| **Very interesting** | hén yǒu yìsǐ | hun yo yee–suh | 很有意思 |
| **Fantastic** | fēicháng hǎo | fay–chahng hao | 非常好 |
| **I really like it.** | Wǒ zhēn xǐhuān. | waw juhn shee–hwan | 我真喜欢 |

ENTERTAINMENT

| ENGLISH | PINYIN | PRONUNCIATION | CHARACTERS |
|---------|--------|---------------|------------|
| **Is there an intermission?** | Yǒu méiyǒu xiūxǐ? | yo may yo shee-oh–shee | 有没有休息？ |
| **Is there a T.V. here?** | Zhèlǐ yǒu diànshì mǎ? | juh–lee yo dee-en–shir mah | 这里有电视吗？ |
| **Television** | diànshì | dee-en–shir | 电视 |
| **Film (movie)** | diànyīng | dee-en–ying | 电影 |
| **Play** | huàjù | hwa–jü | 话剧 |
| **Opera** | gējù | guh jü | 歌剧 |
| **Traditional (Peking) opera** | jīngjù | jing–jü | 京剧 |
| **Variety show** | wényì wǎnhuì | win–yee wahn–hway | 文艺晚会 |
| **Musical evening** | yīnyuè wǎnhuì | yeen–yoo-eh wahn–hway | 音乐晚会 |
| **Acrobats** | zájì | dzah–jee | 杂技 |
| **Martial arts** | wǔshù | woo–shoo | 武术 |
| **Puppet theatre** | mù'ǒuxì | moo-oh–shee | 木偶戏 |
| **Chinese (shadow) boxing** | tàijíquán | tye–jee–chwan | 太极拳 |
| **Sports (competition)** | qiúsài | chee-oh–sye | 球赛 |

| ENGLISH | PINYIN | PRONUNCIATION | CHARACTERS |
|---------|--------|---------------|------------|
| **Theatre** | jùchǎng | ju–chahng | 剧场 |
| **Movie theatre** | diànyǐngyuàn | dee-en–ying yoo-en | 电影院 |
| **Club** | jùlèbù | ju–luh–boo | 俱乐部 |
| **Dance Hall** | wǔtīng | woo–ting | 舞厅 |
| **(To) dance** | tiàowǔ | tee-ow–woo | 跳舞 |
| **Dance** | wǔhuì | woo–hway | 舞会 |
| **Partner** | bàn | ban | 伴 |
| | | | |
| **Chinese film** | zhōngguópiàn | joong–gwaw pee-en | 中国片 |
| **Foreign film** | wàiguópiàn | why–gwaw pee-en | 外国片 |
| **Story (film)** | gùshìpiàn | goo–shir pee-en | 故事片 |
| **Suspense (film)** | jīngxiǎnpiàn | jing–shee-en–pee-en | 惊险片 |
| **Detective (film)** | zhēntànpiàn | juhn–tan–pee-en | 侦探片 |
| **Science Fiction** | kēxué huànxiǎngpiàn | kuh–shoo-eh hwan–shee-ahng–pee-en | 科学幻想片 |
| | | | |
| **Performance** | yǎnchū | yen–choo | 演出 |
| **Act** | jiémù | jee-yeh–moo | 节目 |
| **Program** | jiémùdān/ shuōmíngshū | jee-yeh–moo–dan/ shwaw–ming–shoo | 节目单／说明书 |

| ENGLISH | PINYIN | PRONUNCIATION | CHARACTERS |
|---|---|---|---|
| **Intermission** | xiūxǐ | shee-oh–shee | 休息 |
| **End/finish** | jiéshù | jee-yeh–shoo | 结束 |
| **Sports** | yùndòng | yew-win–doong | 运动 |
| **Ball** | qiú | chee-oh | 球 |
| **Ping Pong** | pīngpāngqiú | ping–pang–chee-oh | 乒乓球 |
| **Basketball** | lánqiú | lahn–chee-oh | 兰球 |
| **Soccer** | zúqiú | dzoo–chee-oh | 足球 |
| **Volley ball** | páiqiú | pie–chee-oh | 排球 |
| **Team** | qiú duì | chee-oh-doo-ay | 球队 |
| **Referee** | cáipànyuán | tseye–pan–yoo-ahn | 裁判员 |
| **Point/goal** | fēn | fun | 分 |
| **(To) win** | yíng | ying | 赢 |
| **(To) lose** | shū | shoo | 输 |
| **One to one** | yì bǐ yī | yee bee yee | 一比一 |
| **One to three** | yì bǐ sān | yee bee san | 一比三 |
| **Four to six** | sì bǐ liù | suh bee lee-oh | 四比六 |
| **Friendship first, competition second** | Yǒuyì dìyī, bǐsài dì'èr | yo–yee dee-yee, bee-sye dee-are | 友谊第一, 比赛第二 |

| ENGLISH | PINYIN | PRONUNCIATION | CHARACTERS |
|---------|--------|---------------|------------|
| **Visit** | cānguān | tsan–gwan | 参观 |
| **Sightsee** | yóulǎn | yo–lahn | 游览 |

## *USEFUL WORDS & PHRASES*

| ENGLISH | PINYIN | PRONUNCIATION | CHARACTERS |
|---------|--------|---------------|------------|
| **How are you?** | Ní hǎo mǎ? | nee hao mah | 你好吗？ |
| **Thank you.** | Xièxiě. | shee-eh shee-eh | 谢谢 |
| **Goodbye.** | Zàijiàn. | dzai–jee-en | 再见 |
| **Welcome.** | Huānyíng. | hwahn–ying | 欢迎 |
| **Simple introduction** | jiǎndāndě jièshào | jee-en–dan–duh–jee-yeh–shao | 简单的介绍 |
| **Good** | hǎo | hao | 好 |
| **Very good** | hén hǎo | hun hao | 很好 |
| **How old are you?** | Nǐ duó dà/ní jǐ suì? | nee dwaw–dah/nee jee–sway | 你多大 / 你几岁？ |
| **Where is the toilet?** | Cèsuǒ zài nálǐ? | tse–swo dzai nah–lee | 厕所在哪里？ |
| **Uncle** | shū-shǔ | shoo–shoo | 叔叔 |

| ENGLISH | PINYIN | PRONUNCIATION | CHARACTERS |
|---------|--------|---------------|------------|
| Aunt | ā–yí | ah–yee | 阿姨 |
| Foreign guest | wàibīn | why–been | 外宾 |
| Foreign friend | wàiguó péngyŏu | why–gwaw pung–yo | 外国朋友 |
| Foreigner | wàiguó rén | why–gwaw run | 外国人 |
| (Let's) go faster! | Kuài yì diăn! | kwhy yee–dee-en | 快一点 |
| (Let's) go slower! | Màn yì diăn! | man yee–dee-en | 慢一点 |
| (Let's) rest! | Xiūxĭ! | shee-oh–shee | 休息 |
| (Please) sit down! | (Qĭng) zuò bă! | (ching) dzwaw–bah | (请) 坐吧 |
| (Let's) go! | Zŏu bă! | dzou–bah | 走吧！ |
| I'm tired. | Wŏ lèi-lĕ. | waw lay–luh | 我累了 |
| Can I take a picture? | Kéyĭ zhàoxiàng mă? | kuh–yee jao-shee-ahng mah? | 可以照象吗？ |
| No more, thank you. (polite refusal of more tea, etc.) | Búyàolĕ, xìexiĕ. | boo–yao–luh, shee-eh shee-eh | 不要了，谢谢 |
| Where is the bus? | Wŏmĕn chē zái năr? | waw–mun cheh dzai nahr | 我们车在哪儿？ |
| Where is our group? | Wŏmĕn tuán zài năr? | waw-mun twahn dzai nahr | 我们团在哪儿？ |

| ENGLISH | PINYIN | PRONUNCIATION | CHARACTERS |
|---|---|---|---|
| I'm lost. | Wǒ mí lùlě. | waw mee–loo-luh | 我迷路了 |
| The children are so cute! | Xiǎo pèngyǒu zhēn kě ǎi! | shee-ow pung–yo juhn kuh–aye | 小朋友真可爱！ |
| Assemble | jíhé | jee huh | 集合 |

## SCHOOLS

| ENGLISH | PINYIN | PRONUNCIATION | CHARACTERS |
|---|---|---|---|
| Primary school | xiǎoxué | shee-ow–shoo-eh | 小学 |
| Primary school student | xiǎoxuéshēng | shee-ow–shoo-eh shung | 小学生 |
| Middle school | zhōngxué | joong–shoo-eh | 中学 |
| Middle school student | zhōngxuéshēng | joong–shoo-eh–shung | 中学生 |
| University | dàxué | dah–shoo-eh | 大学 |
| University student | dàxuéshēng | dah–shoo-eh–shung | 大学生 |
| Institute, college | xuéyuàn | shoo-eh–yoo-ahn | 学院 |
| Teacher's college | shīfàn xuéyuàn | shir–fan shoo-eh–yoo-ahn | 师范学院 |
| Teacher's university | shīfàn dàxué | shir–fan dah–shoo-eh | 师范大学 |
| Medical school | yīxué yuàn | yee–shoo-eh–yoo-ahn | 医学院 |

| ENGLISH | PINYIN | PRONUNCIATION | CHARACTERS |
|---------|--------|---------------|------------|
| **Music school** | yīnyuè xuéyuàn | yeen–yweh shoo-eh–yoo-ahn | 音乐学院 |
| **Art school** | měishù xuéyuàn | may–shoo shoo-eh–yoo-ahn | 美术学院 |
| **Pioneers (children's organization)** | Shăoxiān duì | shao shee-en doo-ay | 少先队 |
| **Communist Youth League (C.Y.L.)** | Gòngqīngtuán | goong–ching–twahn | 共青团 |
| **Communist Youth League member** | Tuányuán | twahn–yoo-ahn | 团员 |
| **Communist Party** | Gòngchándăng | goong–chahn–dahng | 共产党 |
| **Communist Party member** | Dăngyuán | dahng–yoo-ahn | 党员 |
| **Day care center** | tuō'èrsuŏ | too-awe–are–swaw | 托儿所 |

## COMMUNES

| | | | |
|---------|--------|---------------|------------|
| **(People's) commune** | (Rénmín) gōngshè | (run–meen) goong–shuh | （人民）公社 |
| **Production brigade** | dàduì | dah–doo-ay | 大队 |

| ENGLISH | PINYIN | PRONUNCIATION | CHARACTERS |
|---|---|---|---|
| **Production team** | shēngchǎnduì | shung–chahn–doo-ay | 生产队 |
| **Commune member** | shèyuán | shuh–yoo-ahn | 社员 |
| **Male...** | nán... | nan | 男…… |
| **Female...** | nǚ... | nü | 女…… |
| **Peasant/farmer** | nóngmín | noong–meen | 农民 |
| **Poor and lower middle peasant** | pínxiàzhōngnóng | pin–shee-ya–joong–noong | 贫下中农 |
| **Landlord** | dìzhǔ | dee–jew | 地主 |
| **Hospital** | yīyuàn | yee–yoo-ahn | 医院 |
| **Mu (Chinese land measure: 1 mu = 0.164 acre)** | mǔ | moo | 亩 |
| **In agriculture, learn from Dazhai.** | Nóngyè xué dàzhài. | noong–yeh shoo-eh dah–jai | 农业学大寨 |

## FACTORIES

| | | | |
|---|---|---|---|
| **Worker** | gōngrén | goong–run | 工人 |
| **Head of a factory** | chángzhǎng | chahng–jahng | 厂长 |
| **Workshop** | chējiān | cheh–jee-en | 车间 |

| ENGLISH | PINYIN | PRONUNCIATION | CHARACTERS |
|---|---|---|---|
| **Safety and production (a common slogan)** | ānquán shēngchǎn | an–chwan shung–chahn | 安全生产 |
| **In industry, learn from Daqing.** | Gōngyè xué dàqìng. | goong–yeh shoo-eh dah–ching | 工业学大庆 |

## MUSEUMS

| | | | |
|---|---|---|---|
| **Museum** | bówùguǎn | baw–woo–gwan | 博物馆 |
| **Museum of history** | lìshǐ bówùguǎn | lee–shir baw–woo–gwan | 历史博物馆 |
| **Exhibition hall** | zhǎnlánguǎn | jan–lahn–gwan | 展览馆 |
| **Agricultural exhibition hall** | nóngyè zhǎnlánguǎn | noong–yeh jan–lahn–gwan | 农业展览馆 |
| **The Mao Zedong Mausoleum** | Máo Zédōng jìniàntáng | mao dzih–doong jee-nee-en–tahng | 毛泽东纪念堂 |

## SCENIC SITES

| | | | |
|---|---|---|---|
| **Park** | gōngyuán | goong–yoo-ahn | 公园 |
| **Museum** | bówùguǎn | baw–woo–gwan | 博物馆 |

| ENGLISH | PINYIN | PRONUNCIATION | CHARACTERS |
|---------|--------|---------------|------------|
| **Temple** | sìmiào / miào | suh–meow / meow | 寺庙 / 庙 |
| **Pagoda** | tā | tah | 塔 |
| **Ticket** | piào | pee-ow | 票 |
| **Lake** | hú | hoo | 湖 |
| **Hill / mountain** | shān | shan | 山 |
| **River** | hé / jiāng | huh / jee-ahng | 河 / 江 |
| **Boat** | chuán | chwahn | 船 |
| **Pavilion** | tíng | ting | 亭 |
| **Island** | dǎo | dao | 岛 |
| **Cave** | dòng | doong | 洞 |
| **Statue** | sùxiàng | soo–shee-ahng | 塑象 |

## GUANGZHOU

| | | | |
|---------|--------|---------------|------------|
| **Guangzhou (Canton)** | Guǎngzhōu | gwahng–joe | 广州 |
| **Yuehsi Park** | Yuèxiù gōngyuán | yweh–shee-oh goong–yoo-en | 越秀公园 |
| **Liuhua Park** | Liúhuā gōngyuán | lee-oh–hwa goong–yoo-en | 流花公园 |
| **Zhenhai Pavilion Museum** | Zhènhǎilóu bówùguǎn | juhn–hai–lou baw–woo–gwan | 镇海楼博物馆 |

| ENGLISH | PINYIN | PRONUNCIATION | CHARACTERS |
|---------|--------|---------------|------------|
| **Guangzhou Zoo** | Guǎngzhōu dòngwùyuán | gwahng–joe doong-woo–yon | 广州动物园 |
| **Huanghua Martyrs Memorial Park** | Huánghuāgǎng lièshì língyuán | hwahng–hwa–gahng lee-eh–shir ling–yoo-en | 黄花岗烈士陵园 |
| **Shamien** | Shāmiàn | shah–mee-en | 沙面 |
| **Baiyun Mountains (White Cloud Mts)** | Báiyúnshān | bye–yew-win–shan | 白云山 |
| **Outside Guangzhou** | Guǎngzhōu yǐwài | gwahng–joe yee–why | 广州以外 |
| **Foshan city** | Fóshānshì | foh–shan–shir | 佛山市 |
| **Tsunghua Hot Springs** | Cónghuà wēnquán | tsoong–hwa win–chwan | 从化温泉 |
| **Seven Star Crag** | Qīxīngyán | chee–shing–yen | 七星岩 |
| **Zhaoqing city** | Zhàoqìngshì | jao–ching–shir | 肇庆市 |
| **Shenzhen city** | Shēnzhènshì | shun–juhn–shir | 深圳市 |

## BEIJING

| | | | |
|---------|--------|---------------|------------|
| **Beijing (Peking)** | Běijīng | Bay–jing | 北京 |
| **Tianan Men (Square)** | Tiānānmén (guángchǎng) | tee-en–an–mun (gwahng–chahng) | 天安门 (广场 |

| ENGLISH | PINYIN | PRONUNCIATION | CHARACTERS |
|---|---|---|---|
| **Imperial Palace** | Gùgōng | goo–goong | 故宫 |
| **Chienmen** | Qiánmén | chee-en–mun | 前门 |
| **Coal Hill (Park)** | Jĭngshān (gōng-yuán) | jing–shan (goong–yoo-ahn) | 景山（公园） |
| **Peihai (Park)** | Beíhaĭ (gōngyuán) | bay–hai (goong–yoo-ahn) | 北海（公园） |
| **Liuli Alley** | Liúlíchăng | lee-oh–lee–chahng | 琉璃厂 |
| **Chang'an Boulevard** | Cháng'ān dàjiē | chahng–an dah–jee-yeh | 长安大街 |
| **Wang Fu Jing** | Wángfújĭng | wahng–foo–jing | 王府井 |
| **Dongfeng Market** | Dōngfēng shì-chăng | doong–fung shir–chahng | 东风市场 |
| **Summer Palace** | Yìhéyuán | yee–huh–yoo-ahn | 颐和园 |
| **Ming Tombs** | Shísānlíng | shir–san–ling | 十三陵 |
| **Great Wall** | Chángchéng | chahng–chung | 长城 |
| **Great Hall of the People** | Rénmín Dàhuìtáng | run–meen–dah–hway–tahng | 人民大会堂 |

## SHANGHAI

| | | | |
|---|---|---|---|
| **Shanghai** | Shànghaĭ | Shahng–hye | 上海 |

| ENGLISH | PINYIN | PRONUNCIATION | CHARACTERS |
|---------|--------|---------------|------------|
| **The Bund** | Wàitān | why–tan | 外滩 |
| **Yuyuan Market** | Yùyuán shìchǎng | yü–yoo-ahn shih–chahng | 豫园市场 |
| **Hungkou Park** | Hóngkǒu gōngyuán | hoong–kou goong–yoo-ahn | 虹口公园 |
| **Lu Xun Museum** | Lǔ Xùn jìniànguǎn | lü–shwin jee–nee-en-gwan | 鲁迅纪念馆 |
| **Huangpu Wharves** | Huángpǔ mǎtoǔ | hwahng–poo mah–tou | 黄埔码头 |
| **Temple of the Jade Buddha** | Yùfósì | yü–foh–suh | 玉佛寺 |
| **Old City** | Jiùchéng | jee-oh–chung | 旧城 |
| **Nanking Road** | Nánjīnglù | nan–jing–loo | 南京路 |
| **Huaihai Road** | Huáihǎilù | hwhy–hye–loo | 淮海路 |

## GUILIN

| | | | |
|---------|--------|---------------|------------|
| **Guilin (Kweilin)** | Guìlín | Gway–leen | 桂林 |
| **Banyan Lake** | Rónghú | roong–hoo | 榕湖 |
| **Seven Star Hill** | Qīxīngyán | chee–shing–yen | 七星岩 |
| **Reed Flute Cave** | Lúdíyán | loo–dee–yen | 芦笛岩 |
| **Li River** | Líjiāng | lee–jee-ahng | 漓江 |

| **Elephant Nose Hill** | Xiàngbíshān | shee-ahng-bee-shan | 象鼻山 |
| **Yangshuo** | yángshuò | yahng-shwaw | 阳朔 |

## *HANGZHOU*

| **Hangzhou (Hangchow)** | Hángzhōu | hung-joe | 杭州 |
| **West Lake** | Xīhú | shee-hoo | 西湖 |
| **Solitary Hill Island** | Gūshāndǎo | goo-shan-dao | 孤山岛 |
| **Su Tungpo Causeway** | Sūdī | soo-dee | 苏堤 |
| **Viewing Fish at Flower Harbour** | Huāgǎng guānyú | hwa-gahng gwan-yü | 花港观鱼 |
| **Three Pools that Mirror the Moon** | Sāntán yìnyuè | san-tan yeen-yweh | 三潭印月 |
| **Precious Stone Hill** | Bǎoshíshān | bao-shir-shan | 宝石山 |
| **Monastery of the Soul's Retreat** | Língyǐnsì | ling-yeen-suh | 灵隐寺 |
| **The Pagoda of the Six Harmonies** | Liùhétǎ | lee-oh-huh-tah | 六和塔 |
| **Lungjing (Dragon's Well)** | Lóngjǐng | loong-jing | 龙井 |

VISITING/SIGHTSEEING

## NANJING

| ENGLISH | PINYIN | PRONUNCIATION | CHARACTERS |
|---|---|---|---|
| **Nanjing (Nanking)** | Nánjīng | nan–jing | 南京 |
| **Yangtse River** | Chángjiāng | chahng–jee-ahng | 长江 |
| **The Yangtse River Bridge** | Chángjiāng dàqiáo | chahng–jee-ahng dah–chee-ow | 长江大桥 |
| **Hsuanwu Lake** | Xuánwǔhú | shwen–woo-hoo | 玄武湖 |
| **Drum Tower** | Gǔlóu | goo–low | 鼓楼 |
| **Yu Hua Tai (Gardens)** | Yǔhuātái | yü–hwa–tye | 雨花台 |
| **Sun Yatsen's Tomb** | Zhōngshānlíng | joong–shan–ling | 中山陵 |
| **Ling Gu Park** | Línggǔsì | ling–goo–suh | 灵谷寺 |

| ENGLISH | PINYIN | PRONUNCIATION | CHARACTERS |
|---|---|---|---|
| **Professions** | zhíyè | jir–yeh | |
| **What are you?** | Nǐ shì shénmě? | nee shir shummah | 你是什么? |
| **What (work) do you do?** | Nǐ zuò shénmě (gōngzuò)? | nee dzwaw shummah | 你做什么（工作）？ |
| **I am a...** | Wǒ shì (yígě)... | waw shir (yee–guh)... | 我是(一个)...... |
| **Actor/actress** | yǎnyuán | yen–yoo-ahn | 演员 |
| **Administrative official** | xíngzhèng gànbù | shing–junhg gahn–boo | 行政干部 |
| **Banker** | yínhángjiā | ying–hung–jee-ah | 银行家 |
| **Businessman/woman** | shāngrén | shahng–run | 商人 |
| **Cadre** | gànbù | gahn–boo | 干部 |
| **Capitalist** | zīběnjiā | dzih–bun–jee-ah | 资本家 |
| **Consultant** | shāngyìzhě | shahng–yee–juh | 商议者 |
| **Director (cinema)** | dáoyǎn | dao–yen | 导演 |
| **Doctor** | yīshēng/dàifů | yee–shung/dye–foo | 医生 / 大夫 |
| **Driver (of taxis, buses, trucks, etc.)** | sījī | suh–jee | 司机 |

| ENGLISH | PINYIN | PRONUNCIATION | CHARACTERS |
|---|---|---|---|
| **Dancer** | wúdǎojiā | woo–dao–jee-ah | 舞蹈家 |
| **Editor** | biānjí | bee-en–jee | 编辑 |
| **Engineer** | gōngchéngshī | goong–chung–shir | 工程师 |
| **Factoryhead** | chángzhǎng | chahng–jahng | 厂长 |
| **Foreman** | chējiān zhǔrèn | cheh–jee-en jew–run | 车间主任 |
| **Group (or delegation) leader** | tuánzhǎng | twahn–jahng | 团长 |
| **Guide** | xiángdǎo/péitóng | shee-ang–dao/pay-toong | 向导 / 陪同 |
| **High level cadre** | gāojí gànbù | gao–jee gahn–boo | 高级干部 |
| **Housewife** | jiātíng fùnǚ | jee-ah–ting foo-nü | 家庭妇女 |
| **Intellectual** | zhīshǐ fènzǐ | jir–shir fun–dzih | 知识分子 |
| **Journalist** | jìzhě | jee–juh | 记者 |
| **Lawyer** | lǜshī | lü–shir | 律师 |
| **Lecturer** | jiǎngshī | jee-ahng–shir | 讲师 |
| **Librarian** | túshūguǎn guánlǐyuán | too–shoo–gwan–gwan–lee–yoo-ahn | 图书馆管理员 |
| **Member of the Central Committee** | Zhōngyāng wěiyuán | joong–yahng way–yoo-ahn | 中央委员 |
| **Musician** | yīnyuèjiā | yeen–yweh jee-ah | 音乐家 |
| **Nurse** | hùshì | hoo–shir | 护士 |

| ENGLISH | PINYIN | PRONUNCIATION | CHARACTERS |
|---|---|---|---|
| **Peasant/farmer** | nóngmín | noong–meen | 农民 |
| **Photographer** | shèyīngshī | sheh–ying–shir | 摄影师 |
| **Policeman/woman** | jǐngchá | jing–cha | 警察 |
| **Politburo member** | zhèngzhìjú wěiyuán | juhng–jir–jü way–yoo-ahn | 政治局委员 |
| **Politician** | zhèngzhìjiā | juhng–jir–jee-ah | 政治家 |
| **Professor** | jiàoshòu | je-ow–show | 教授 |
| **Researcher** | yánjiūzhě | yen–jee-oh–juh | 研究者 |
| **Research student** | yánjiūshēng | yen–jee-oh–shung | 研究生 |
| **Retired** | tuìxiū | too-ay–shee-oh | 退休 |
| **Sailor** | shuíshǒu | shway–show | 水手 |
| **Salesperson** | shòuhuòyuán | show–hwa–yoo-ahn | 售货员 |
| **Scientist** | kēxuéjiā | kuh shoo-eh–jee-ah | 科学家 |
| **Secretary (office)** | mìshū | mee–shoo | 秘书 |
| **Secretary (party, committee, other organization)** | shūjì | shoo–jee | 书记 |
| **Shopkeeper** | diànzhǔ | dee-en–jew | 店主 |
| **Singer** | gēshǒu | guh–show | 歌手 |
| **Soldier/P.L.A. (man)** | bīng/jiěfàngjūn | bing/jee-yeh fung–jwin | 兵／解放军 |

PROFESSIONS

| ENGLISH | PINYIN | PRONUNCIATION | CHARACTERS |
|---------|--------|---------------|------------|
| **Student** | xuéshēng | shoo-eh–shung | 学生 |
| **Teacher** | jiàoyuán/lǎoshī | jee-ow–yoo-ahn/lao–shir | 教员 / 老师 |
| **Technician** | jìshù rényuán | jee–shoo run–yoo-ahn | 技术人员 |
| **Ticket seller** | shòupiàoyuán | show–pee-ow–yoo-ahn | 售票员 |
| **Tourist** | yóukè/lǚkè | yo–kuh/lü–kuh | 遊客 / 旅客 |
| **Translator** | fānyìzhě | fan–yee–juh | 翻译者 |
| **Unemployed** | dàiyè/shīyè | dye–yeh/shir–yeh | 待业 / 失业 |
| **Worker** | gōngrén | goong–run | 工人 |
| **...worker/one who works in...** | ...gōngzuòzhě | goong–dzraw–juh | ……工作者 |
| **Writer** | zuòjiā | dzraw–jee-ah | 作家 |

| ENGLISH | PINYIN | PRONUNCIATION | CHARACTERS |
|---|---|---|---|
| **Shopping** | gōuwù | go-woo | 购物 |
| **I want...** | Wǒ yào... | waw yao | 我要…… |
| **I want (to buy)...** | Wǒ yào mǎi... | waw yao my | 我要买…… |
| **I want that one.** | Wǒ yào nèigě. | waw yao nay–guh | 我要那个 |
| **I want to look at...** | Wǒ yào kàn... | waw yao–kahn | 我要看…… |
| **Do you have any others?** | Yǒu biédě mǎ? | yo bee-eh-duh mah | 有别的吗？ |
| **Can I try it?** | Kéyǐ shì yíxià? | kuh–yee shir yee–shee-ya | 可以试一下？ |
| **Where can I get...?** | Nálǐ/nǎr kéyí mǎi...? | nah–lee/nahr kuh–yee my | 哪里 / 哪儿可以买…？ |
| **Do you have (any)...?** | Yǒu méiyǒu...? | yo may yo... | 有没有…？ |
| **A little bigger** | dà yì diǎn | dah yee–dee-en | 大一点 |
| **A little smaller** | xiǎo yì diǎn | shee-ow yee–dee-en | 小一点 |
| **It doesn't fit.** | Zhè bù héshì. | juh boo huh–shir | 这不合适 |
| **Too** | tài | tye | 太 |

| ENGLISH | PINYIN | PRONUNCIATION | CHARACTERS |
|---------|--------|---------------|------------|
| **Expensive** | guì | gway | 贵 |
| **Cheap** | piányǐ | pee-en—yee | 便宜 |
| **One (item)** | yígě | yee-guh | 一个 |
| **Two (items), etc.** | liănggě | lee-ahng—guh | 两个 |
| **Tight/loose** | jǐn / sōng | jeen/soong | 紧 / 松 |
| **Short/long** | duăn/cháng | dwan/chahng | 短 / 长 |

## SHOPS

| | | | |
|---|---|---|---|
| **Store** | shāngdiàn | shahng dee-en | 商店 |
| **Department Store** | băihuò shāngdiàn | bye-hwaw shahng—dee-en | 百货商店 |
| **Friendship Store** | yŏuyì shāngdiàn | yo-yee shahng—dee-en | 友谊商店 |
| **Bookstore** | shūdiàn | shoo-dee-en | 书店 |
| **Antique Shop** | gúdŏng shāngdiàn | goo-doong shahng—dee-en | 古董商店 |
| **Painting Shop** | shùhuà diàn | shoo-hwa dee-en | 书画店 |
| **Souvenir Shop** | jìniànpīn diàn | jee-nee-en-peen dee-en | 纪念品店 |

| | | | |
|---|---|---|---|
| **Food Store** | shípǐn shāngdiàn | shir–peen shahng–dee-en | 食品商店 |
| **Market** | shìchǎng | shir–chahng | 市场 |
| **Small Shop (in hotel)** | xiǎomàibù | shee-ow–my–boo | 小卖部 |
| **Barber** | lǐfà diàn | lee–fah dee-en | 理发店 |
| **Stationery Store** | wénjù shāngdiàn | win–jü shahng–dee-en | 文具商店 |
| **Hat Shop** | màozǐ diàn | mao–dzih dee-en | 帽子店 |
| **Shoe Shop** | xiédiàn | shee-eh dee-en | 鞋店 |
| **Clothing Shop/Tailors** | fúzhuāngdiàn | foo–jew-ahng–dee-en | 服装店 |

## CLOTHES

| | | | |
|---|---|---|---|
| **Clothes** | yīfú | yee–foo | 衣服 |
| **Cap** | màozǐ | mao–dzih | 帽子 |
| **Mao cap** | jūnmào (lit. "army cap") | jwin–mao | 军帽 |
| **Shirt** | chènshān | chun–shan | 衬衫 |
| **Pants** | kùzǐ | koo–dzih | 裤子 |
| **Track suit** | yùndòngyī | yew-win–doong–yee | 运动衣 |
| **Socks** | wàzǐ | wah–dzih | 袜子 |

CLOTHES

| ENGLISH | PINYIN | PRONUNCIATION | CHARACTERS |
|---|---|---|---|
| **Underpants** | nèikù | nay–koo | 内裤 |
| **Undershirt** | bèixīn | bay–sheen | 背心 |
| **Bra** | rǔzhào | roo–jao | 乳罩 |
| **Scarf** | wéijīn | way–jeen | 围巾 |
| **Gloves** | shǒutào | show–tao | 手套 |
| **Handkerchief** | shǒujuàn | show–jwan | 手绢 |
| **Mao jacket** | zhōngshānzhuāng | joong–shan–jew-ahng | 中山装 |
| **Overcoat** | dàyī | dah–yee | 大衣 |
| | | | |
| **Shoes (a pair)** | xiézǐ (yì shuāng) | shee-eh–dzih (yee shwahng) | 鞋子 (一双) |
| **Cloth shoes** | bùxié | boo–shee-eh | 布鞋 |
| **(Plastic) Sandals** | (sùliào) liángxié | (soo–lee-ow) lee-ahng–shee-eh | (塑料) 凉鞋 |
| **Boots** | xuēzǐ | shoo-eh–dzih | 靴子 |
| | | | |
| **Shoulder bag** | shūbāo | shoo–bao | 书包 |
| **Traveling bag** | lǚxíngbāo | lü–shing–bao | 旅行包 |
| **Red star badge** | hóngxīng huīzhāng | hoong–shing hway–jahng | 红星徽章 |

| **Mao badge** | Máo zhǔxí xiàngzhāng | Mao jew-shee shee-ahng-jahng | 毛主席象章 |

## COLORS

| English | Pinyin | Pronunciation | Characters |
|---|---|---|---|
| **Color** | yánsè · | yen-se | 颜色 |
| **Dark** | shēn | shun | 深 |
| **Light** | qiān/dàn | chee-en/dan | 浅／淡 |
| **Black** | hēi (dě) | hay (duh) | 黑（的） |
| **White** | bái (dě) | bye (duh) | 白（的） |
| **Blue** | lán (dě) | lahn (duh) | 兰（的） |
| **Green** | lǜ (dě) | lü (duh) | 绿（的） |
| **Red** | hóng (dě) | hoong (duh) | 红（的） |
| **Yellow** | huáng (dě) | hwahng (duh) | 黄（的） |
| **Purple** | zǐsè (dě) | dzih-suh (duh) | 紫色（的） |
| **Brown** | kāfēisè (dě) | kay-fay-suh (duh) | 咖啡色（的） |
| **Pink** | fēnhóng (dě) | fun-hoong (duh) | 纷红（的） |
| **Orange** | júzǐsè (dě) | jü-dzih-suh (duh) | 橘子色（的） |
| **Beige** | mǐsè (dě) | mee-suh (duh) | 米色（的） |

COLORS

| ENGLISH | PINYIN | PRONUNCIATION | CHARACTERS |
|---------|--------|---------------|------------|

## *SOUVENIRS*

| ENGLISH | PINYIN | PRONUNCIATION | CHARACTERS |
|---------|--------|---------------|------------|
| **Souvenir** | jìniànpǐn | jee–nee–en–peen | 纪念品 |
| **Local specialties/ products** | túchǎn/tèchǎn | too–chahn/tuh–chahn | 土产/ 特产 |
| **Antique** | gúdǒng | goo–doong | 古董 |
| **Art work** | yìshúpǐn | yee–shoo–peen | 艺术品 |
| **Mass-produced art works** | gōngyìpǐn | goong–yee–peen | 工艺品 |
| **Book** | shū | shoo | 书 |
| **Picture book** | huàcè | hwa–tsuh | 画册 |
| **Handicraft** | shǒugōngyìpǐn | show–goong yee–peen | 手工艺品 |
| **Painting** | huà | hwa | 画 |
| **(Chinese) painting** | zhōngguóhuà | joong–gwaw–hwa | 中国画 |
| **Chinese brush** | máobǐ | mao–bee | 毛笔 |
| **Pottery** | taócí/táoqì | tao–tsih/tao–chee | 陶瓷/ 陶器 |
| **Porcelain** | cíqì | tsih–chee | 瓷器 |
| **Teapot** | cháhú | cha–hoo | 茶壶 |
| **Teacup** | chábēi | cha–bay | 茶杯 |
| **Tea** | chá | cha | 茶 |

| **Jewelry** | shǒushì | show–shir | 首饰 |
| **Silk** | sīchóu | suh–chou | 丝绸 |
| **Rug** | dìtǎn | dee–tan | 地毯 |
| **Jade/of jade** | yù/yùdě | yü/yü–duh | 玉 / 玉的 |
| **Lacquerware** | qīqì | chee–chee | 漆器 |
| **Abacus** | suànpán/zhūpán | soo-ahn–pan/jew–pan | 算盘 / 珠盘 |
| **Papercut** | jiánzhǐ | jee-en–jir | 剪纸 |
| **Woodblock print** | bǎnhuà | ban–hwa | 版画 |

## HOTEL STORE

| **Hotel Store** | xiǎomàibù | shee-ow–my–boo | 小卖部 |
| | | | |
| **Fruit** | shuíguǒ | shway–gwaw | 水果 |
| **Apple** | píngguǒ | ping–gwaw | 苹果 |
| **Pear** | lí | lee | 梨 |
| **Peach** | taózǐ | tao–dzih | 桃子 |
| **Pineapple** | bōluó | baw–lwaw | 菠萝 |
| **Persimmon** | shìzǐ | shir–dzih | 柿子 |
| **Orange** | júzǐ | jü–dzih | 橘子 |

| ENGLISH | PINYIN | PRONUNCIATION | CHARACTERS |
|---|---|---|---|
| **Mandarin orange** | gān | gahn | 柑 |
| **Watermelon** | xīguā | shee–gwah | 西瓜 |
| **Lychee** | lìzhī | lee–jir | 荔枝 |
| **Grape** | pútåo | poo–tao | 葡萄 |
| **Dried Fruit** | shuíguŏgān | shway–gwaw–gahn | 水果干 |
| **Candies** | táng | tahng | 糖 |
| **Chocolate** | qiăokèlì | chee-ow kuh–lee | 巧克力 |
| **Bubble-gum** | kŏuxiāngtáng | kou–shee-ahng–tahng | 口香糖 |
| **Biscuits** | bīnggān | bing–gahn | 饼干 |
| **Beer** | píjiŭ | pee–jee-oh | 啤酒 |
| **Soft drink** | qìshuĭ | chee–shway | 汽水 |
| **Wine** | jiŭ | jee-oh | 酒 |
| **Grape wine** | pútåojiŭ | poo–tao–jee-oh | 葡萄酒 |
| **Chinese wine** | báijiŭ | bye–jee-oh | 白酒 |
| **Maotai wine** | máotáijiŭ | mao-tye–jee-oh | 茅台酒 |
| **Mineral water** | kuàngshānshuĭ | kwahng–shan–shway | 矿山水 |
| **Cigarette** | xiāngyān/yān | shee-ahng–yen/yen | 香烟/ 烟 |

| ENGLISH | PINYIN | PRONUNCIATION | CHARACTERS |
|---|---|---|---|
| Cigar | xuějiā | shoo-eh–jee-ah | 雪茄 |
| Pipe tobacco | yāncǎo | yen–tsao | 烟草 |
| Matches | huǒchái | hwaw–chai | 火柴 |
| Lighter | dáhuǒjí | dah–hwaw–jee | 打火机 |
| Lighter Fluid | qìyóu | chee–yo | 汽油 |

## TOILETRIES

| | | | |
|---|---|---|---|
| Toiletries | huàzhuāngyòngpǐn | hwa–jew-ahng yoong–peen | 化妆用品 |
| Toothpaste | yágāo | yah–gao | 牙膏 |
| Toothbrush | yáshuā | yah–shwah | 牙刷 |
| Mirror | jìngzǐ | jing–dzih | 镜子 |
| Comb | shūzǐ | shoo–dzih | 梳子 |
| Soap | féizào | fay–dzao | 肥皂 |
| Shampoo | xǐfáfěn | shee–fah–fun | 洗发粉 |
| Lipstick | koǔhóng | koe–hoong | 口红 |
| Cream | gāo | gao | 膏 |
| Perfume | xiāngshuǐ | shee-ahng–shway | 香水 |
| Cosmetics | huàzhuāngpǐn | hwa–jew-ahng–peen | 化粧品 |
| Razor-blade | dāopiàn | dao–pee-en | 刀片 |
| Talcum powder | shuǎngshēnfěn | shwahng–shen–fun | 爽身粉 |

| ENGLISH | PINYIN SPELLING | PRONUNCIATION | CHARACTERS |
| --- | --- | --- | --- |
| **Ankle** | guǒ | gwaw | 踝 |
| **Arm** | gēbǒ | guh–baw | 胳膊 |
| **Back** | bèi | bay | 背 |
| **Bladder** | pángguāng | pahng–gwahng | 膀胱 |
| **Blood** | xuě | shoo-eh | 血 |
| **Bone** | gǔtóu | goo–toe | 骨头 |
| **Bowels** | chángbù | chahng–boo | 肠部 |
| **Breast** | xiōng | shee-ong | 胸 |
| **Buttocks** | pìgǔ | pee–goo | 屁股 |
| **Cheek** | miànjiá | mee-an-jee-ah | 面颊 |
| **Chest** | xiōngtáng | shee-ong–tahng | 胸膛 |
| **Chin** | xiàbǎ | shee-ya–bah | 下巴 |
| **Ear** | ěrduǒ | are–dwaw | 耳朵 |
| **Elbow** | gēbǒ zhǒu | guh–bay joe | 胳膊肘 |
| **Eye** | yǎnjǐng | yen–jing | 眼睛 |
| **Face** | liǎn | lee-en | 脸 |
| **Finger** | shóuzhǐ | show–jir | 手指 |

| ENGLISH | PINYIN | PRONUNCIATION | CHARACTERS |
|---------|--------|---------------|------------|
| **Foot** | jiǎo | jee-ow | 脚 |
| **Forehead** | qián'é | chee-an–uh | 前额 |
| **Hand** | shǒu | show | 手 |
| **Head** | tóu | toe | 头 |
| **Heart** | xīnzàng | sheen–dzahng | 心脏 |
| **Heel** | zhǒng | joong | 踵 |
| **Hip** | péngǔ | pun–goo | 盆骨 |
| **Intestines** | chángzǐ | chahng–dzih | 肠子 |
| **Jaw** | xià'è | shee-ya–uh | 下颚 |
| **Kidney** | shèn | shun | 肾 |
| **Knee** | xī | shee | 膝 |
| **Kneecap** | xīgài | shee–gai | 膝盖 |
| **Leg** | tuǐ | too-ay | 腿 |
| **Lip** | zuǐchún | dzway–chwin | 咀唇 |
| **Liver** | gān | gahn | 肝 |
| **Lungs** | fèi | fay | 肺 |
| **Mouth** | zuǐ (bǎ) | dzway (bah) | 咀（巴） |
| **Muscle** | jīròu | jee–row | 肌肉 |
| **Neck** | bózǐ | baw–dzih | 脖子 |

| | ENGLISH | PINYIN | PRONUNCIATION | CHARACTERS |
|---|---|---|---|---|
| **Nerves** | shénjīng | shun–jing | 神经 |
| **Nose** | bízǐ | bee–dzih | 鼻子 |
| **Rib** | leìgǔ | lay–goo | 肋骨 |
| **Shoulder** | jiān (bǎng) | jee-en (bahng) | 肩膀 |
| **Skin** | pífū | pee–foo | 皮肤 |
| **Spine** | jíliǎnggǔ | jee–lee-ahng–goo | 脊梁骨 |
| **Stomach** | dùzí | doo–dzih | 肚子 |
| **Teeth** | yáchǐ | yah–chir | 牙齿 |
| **Thigh** | dà tuǐ | dah–too-ay | 大腿 |
| **Throat** | hóulóng | hou–loong | 喉咙 |
| **Thumb** | múzhǐ | moo–jir | 拇指 |
| **Toe** | jiáozhǐ | jee-ow–jir | 脚指 |
| **Tongue** | shétou | shuh–toe | 舌头 |
| **Tonsils** | biǎntáoxiàn | bee-en–tao–shee-en | 扁桃腺 |
| **Urine** | niào | nee-ow | 尿 |
| **Vein** | xuéguān | shoo-eh–gwan | 血管 |
| **Wrist** | shǒu wànzǐ | show wahn–dzih | 手腕子 |

| *ENGLISH* | *PINYIN* | *PRONUNCIATION* | *CHARACTERS* |
|---|---|---|---|
| **Left** | zuŏ | dzwaw | 左 |
| **Right** | yòu | yo | 右 |
| **Top** | shàngbiǎn | shahng–bee-en | 上边 |
| **Bottom** | xiàbiǎn | shee-ya–bee-en | 下边 |
| **Inside** | lībiǎn | lee–bee-en | 里边 |
| **Outside** | wàibiǎn | why–bee-en | 外边 |

| ENGLISH | PINYIN | PRONUNCIATION | CHARACTERS |
|---------|--------|---------------|------------|
| **Doctor** | yīshēng / daìfǔ | yee–shung / dye–foo | 医生 / 大夫 |
| **Nurse** | hùshì | hoo–shir | 护士 |
| **Hospital** | yīyuàn | yee–yoo-ahn | 医院 |
| **Clinic** | yīliàosuǒ | yee–lee-ow–swo | 医疗所 |
| **I'm not feeling well.** | Wǒ bù shūfú. | waw boo shoo–foo | 我不舒服 |
| **I'm sick.** | Wǒ bìnglě. | waw bing–luh | 我病了 |
| **I'd like to see a doctor.** | Wǒ yào kàn yīshēng. | waw yao kahn yee–shung | 我要看医生 |
| **It's serious.** | Shì yánzhòng. | shir yen–joong | 是严重 |
| **It's an emergency.** | Shì jíshì. | shir jee–shir | 是急事 |
| **Please hurry.** | Qǐng kuài yìdiǎn. | ching kwhy yee–dee-en | 请快一点 |
| **I have a fever.** | Wǒ fāshāolě. | waw fah–shao–luh | 我发烧了 |
| **I feel weak.** | Wǒ juédě ruǎnruò. | waw jweh–duh roo-an–roo-waw | 我觉得软弱 |
| **I've been throwing up.** | Wǒ tùlě. | waw too–luh | 我吐了 |

| ENGLISH | PINYIN | PRONUNCIATION | CHARACTERS |
|---------|--------|---------------|------------|
| **My stomach is upset.** | Wǒ dùzǐ bù shūfú. | waw doo–dzih boo shoo–foo | 我肚子不舒服 |
| **I feel dizzy.** | Wǒ juédě tóu yūn. | waw jweh–duh tou–yew-win | 我觉得头晕 |
| **It hurts here.** | Wǒ zhèr téng. | waw jar tung | 我这儿疼 |
| **My...hurts** | Wǒde...téng | waw–duh...tung | 我的…疼 |
| **I can't move my...** | Wǒ bù néng dòng wǒde... | waw boo–nung doong waw–duh... | 我不能动我的…… |
| **It's probably...** | Dàgài shì... | dah–guy shir | 大概是…… |
| **It might be...** | Kěnéng shì... | kuh–nung shir | 可能是…… |
| **It's just...** | Zhǐ shì... | jir shir | 只是…… |
| **It's nothing serious.** | Méi shénmě shì. | may shummah shir | 没什么事 |
| **Is it serious?** | Shì yánzhòng mǎ? | shir yen–joong mah | 是严重吗？ |
| **Can I continue to travel?** | Néng bù néng jìxù lǚxíng? | nung boo–nung jee–shoo lü–shing | 能不能继续旅行？ |
| **I feel better.** | Hǎo yìdiǎnlě. | hao yee–dee-en–luh | 好一点了 |
| **I feel worse.** | Gèng bù shūfú. | gung boo shoo–foo | 更不舒服 |
| **Much the same** | háishì nèiyàng | hye–shir nay–yahng | 还是那样 |

**SEEING THE DOCTOR**

| ENGLISH | PINYIN | PRONUNCIATION | CHARACTERS |
|---|---|---|---|
| **Allergy** | guòmǐn (zhèng) | gwaw–meen (juhng) | 过敏（症） |
| **Bruise/wound** | shānghén | shahng hun | 伤痕 |
| **Burn** | shāoshāng | shao–shahng | 烧伤 |
| **Chill** | shòu hánlě | show han–luh | 受寒了 |
| **Cramp** | chōujīn | chou jeen | 抽筋 |
| **Cough** | késòu | kuh–sow | 咳嗽 |
| **Cold/flu** | gǎnmào | gahn–mao | 感冒 |
| **Diarrhoea** | lādùzǐ | la doo–dzih | 拉肚子 |
| **Fever** | fāshāo | fah shao | 发烧 |
| **Headache** | tóuténg | toe tuhng | 头疼 |
| **Illness** | bìng | bing | 病 |
| **Infection** | chuánrǎn | chwahng–ran | 传染 |
| **Itch** | yǎng | yahng | 痒 |
| **Nausea** | ěxīn | uh–sheen | 恶心 |
| **Pain** | téng | tuhng | 疼 |
| **Rheumatism** | fēngshī (zhèng) | fung–shir (juhng) | 风湿（症） |
| **Sore throat** | hóulóng téng | hou–loong tuhng | 喉咙疼 |
| **Toothache** | yáchī téng | yah–chir tuhng | 牙齿疼 |
| **Ulcer** | kuìyáng | kway–yahng | 溃疡 |

| ENGLISH | PINYIN | PRONUNCIATION | CHARACTERS |
|---|---|---|---|
| **I'm diabetic.** | Wó yŏu táng-niàobìng. | waw yo tahng-nee-ow-bing | 我有糖尿病 |
| **I've a heart condition.** | Wó yŏu xīnzang bing. | waw yo sheen-dzahng-bing | 我有心脏病 |
| **I'm allergic to...** | Wŏ duì...yŏu guòmīn fǎnyīng. | waw doo-ay... yo gwaw-meen fan-ying | 我对……有 过敏反应 |
| **This is my usual medicine.** | Zhèi shì wŏ chīdě yào. | jay shir waw chir-duh yao | 这是我吃 的药 |
| **I need this medicine.** | Wŏ xūyào zhei zhŏng yào. | waw shoo-yao jay joong yao | 我需要这 种药 |
| **What kind of medicine is this?** | Zhèi shì něi yìzhŏng yào? | jay shir nay yee-joong yao | 这是哪一 种药？ |
| **How should I take it?** | Gāi zěnmě chī? | guy dzummah chir | 该怎么吃？ |
| **Once/twice/three times a day** | měitiān yī/liǎng/sān cì | may tee-en yee/lee-ahng/san-tsih | 每天一/ 两/三次 |
| **Two tablets each time** | (měi) yīcì liǎng-gě | (may) yee-tsih lee-ahng/guh | （每）一次 两个 |
| **Is it necessary?** | Shì búshì bìyàodě? | shir boo-shir bee-yao-duh | 是不是必要 的？—— |

**SEEING THE DOCTOR**

| ENGLISH | PINYIN | PRONUNCIATION | CHARACTERS |
|---------|--------|---------------|------------|
| **How much does/will it cost?** | Shì duóshǎo qián? | shir dwaw–shao chee–en | 是多少钱？ |
| **Western medicine** | xīyào | shee–yao | 西药 |
| **Chinese medicine** | zhōngyào | joong–yao | 中药 |
| **Acupuncture** | zhēnjiù | juhn–jee-oh | 针灸 |
| **Antibiotic** | kàngshēngsù | kahng-shung-soo | 抗生素 |
| **Aspirin** | āsīpīlín | ah–suh–pee–leen | 阿斯匹林 |
| **Bandage** | bēngdài | bung–dye | 绷带 |
| **Blood pressure** | xuěyā | shoo-eh–yah | 血压 |
| **High/low** | gāo/dī | gao/dee | 高 / 低 |
| **Operation** | dòng shǒushù | doong show–shoo | 动手术 |
| **Pill** | yàopiàn/yàowán | yao–pee-en/ yao–wahn | 药片 / 药丸 |
| **Pulse** | màibó | my–baw | 脉膊 |
| **Fast/slow** | kuài/màn | kwhy/man | 快 / 慢 |
| **Prescription** | yàofāng | yao–fahng | 药方 |
| **Injection** | dǎ zhēn | dah–juhn | 打针 |
| **X-ray** | tòushì | toe–shir | 透视 |
| **Tranquilizer** | āndìng yào | an-ding–yao | 安定药 |
| **Sleeping pills** | ānmián yào | an–mee-en–yao | 安眠药 |

# COMMON SLOGANS & POLITICAL EXPRESSIONS

**We have friends all over the world.**
Wŏmĕndĕ péngyŏu biān tiānxià.
waw–mun–duh pung–yo bee-en–tee-en shee-ya

我们的朋友遍天下

**Long live the friendship between the people of China and…**
Zhōng…rénmín zhījiāndĕ yŏuyì wànsuì!
joong…run–meen jir–jee-en–duh yo–yee wahn–sway!

中……人民之间
的友谊万岁！

| **America** | Mĕi | may | 美 |
| **Australia** | Ào | ow | 澳 |
| **Canada** | Jiā | jee-ah | 加 |
| **England** | Yīng | ying | 英 |
| **Japan** | Rì | rih | 日 |
| **France** | Fā | fah | 法 |
| **Germany** | Dé | duh | 德 |
| **Italy** | Yì | yee | 意 |

**Friendship first, competition second**
Yǒuyì dìyī, bǐsài dì'èr
yo–yee dee–yee, bee–sye dee–are

友谊第一，比赛第二

**Serve the People.**
Wèi rénmín fúwù.
way run–meen foo–wo

为人民服务

**Long live friendship!**
Yǒuyì wànsuì!
yo–yee wahn–sway!

友谊万岁！

**Long live...!**
...wànsuì!
...wahn–sway!

……万岁！

**Self-reliance**
Zìlì gēng shēng
dzih–lee–gung–shung

自力更生

**Long live the unity of the peoples of the world!**　　全世界人民大团结万岁!
Quán shìjiè rénmín dà tuánjié wànsuì!
chwan shir–jee-yeh run–meen dah twahn–jee-eh wahn-sway!

**Workers of the world unite!**　　全世界无产者联合起来!
Quán shìjiè wúchánzhě liánhé qǐlái!
chwan shir–jee-yeh woo–chan–juh lee-en–huh chee–lye!

**Long live Marxism, Leninism, and Mao Zedong Thought!**
Mǎkèsīzhǔyì, Lièníngzhǔyì, Máo Zédóng Sīxiǎng Wànsuì!
mah–kuh–suh–jew-yee, lee-eh–ning–jew–yee, mao–dzuh–doong suh–shee-ahng
 wahn–sway　　马克思主义、列宁主义、毛泽东思想万岁!

**Long live the great, glorious, and correct Communist Party of China!**
Wěidàdě, guāngróngdě, Zhèngquèdě Zhōngguó gòngchándǎng wànsuì!
way–dah–duh, gwahng–roong–duh, juhng–chyweh–duh joong–gwaw
 goong–chahn–dahng wahn–sway　　伟大的、光荣的、正确的中国共产党万岁!

**Long live the Great Proletarian Cultural Revolution!**
Wénhuà dà gémìng wànsuì!
win–hwa dah guh–ming wahn–sway

无产阶级文化大革命万岁!

**Learn from Daqing in industry!**
Gōngyè xué Dàqìng!
goong–yeh shoo-eh dah–ching

工业学大庆

**Learn from Dazhai in agriculture!**
Nóngyè xué Dàzhài!
noong–yeh shoo-eh dah–jai

农业学大寨

**Develop the economy, ensure supply!**
Fāzhǎn jīngjì, bǎozhàng gōngyìng!
fah–jan jing–jee, bao–juhng goong–ying

发展经济、保障供给

**Science means eternal spring!**
Kēxué yóngyuǎn shì chūntiān!
kuh–shoo-eh yoong–yoo-ahn shir chwin–tee-en

科学永远是春天

**The Four Modernizations**
Sìgè xiàndàihuà (sihua)
suh–guh shee-en–dye–hwa (suh–hwa)

四个现代化（四化）

**Liberation**
Jiěfàng
jee-yeh–fahng

解放

**Before liberation**
jiěfàng yǐquán
jee-yeh–fahng yee-tee-en

解放以前

**After liberation**
Jiěfàngyǐhòu
jee-yeh–fahng yee–hoe

解放以后

**The Great Leap Forward (1958)**
Dà yuèjìn
dah yweh–jeen

大跃进

**The Cultural Revolution (1966–76)**    文化大革命（文化革命）
Wén huà dà gémìng (wénhuà gémìng)
win–hwa dah guh–ming (win–hwa guh–ming)

**Before the Cultural Revolution**    文化革命以前
Wén huà gémìng yīquán
win–hwa guh–ming yee–tee-en

**After the Cultural Revolution**    文化革命以后
Wénhuà gémìng yīhòu
win–hwa guh–ming yee–hoe

**The April 5 Movement (the Tiananmen Incident)**    四·五运动（天安门事件）
Sìwǔ yùndòng (Tiānānmén Shìjiàn)
suh–woo yew-win–doong (tee-en–an–mun shir–jee-en)

**Xidan Democracy Wall**    西单民主墙
Xīdān mínzhū qiáng
shee–dan meen–jew–chee-ahng

**Democracy and legality**
Mínzhǔ yú fǎzhì
meen–jew yü fah–jir

民主与法制

**Human rights**
Rénquán
run chwan

人权

**Stability and unity**
Āndìng tuánjié
an–ding twahn–jee-yeh

安定团结

# *FAMOUS PEOPLE*

## *POLITICAL*

| | | | |
|---|---|---|---|
| **Mao Zedong (Mao Tsetung)** | Máo Zédōng | mao dzuh–doong | 毛泽东 |
| **Chairman Mao** | Máo zhǔxí | mao jew–shee | 毛主席 |
| **Zhou Enlai (Chou En-lai)** | Zhōu Ēnlái | joe en–lye | 周恩来 |
| **Premier Zhou** | Zhōu zǒnglǐ | joe dzoong–lee | 周总理 |
| **Zhu De (Chu Teh)** | Zhū Dé | jew duh | 朱德 |
| **Sun Zhongshan (Sun Yat-sen)** | Sūn Zhōngshān | swun joong–shan | 孙中山 |
| **Hua Guofeng (Hua Kuo-feng)** | Huà Guófēng | hwa gwaw–fung | 华国锋 |
| **Chairman Hua** | Huà zhǔxí | hwa jew–shee | 华主席 |
| **Deng Xiaoping (Teng Hsiao-ping)** | Dèng Xiǎopíng | dung shee-ow–ping | 邓小平 |
| **Vice-Chairman Deng** | Dèng fùzhǔxí | dung foo–jew-shee | 邓付主席 |
| **Ye Jianying (Yeh Chien-ying)** | Yè Jiànyīng | yeh jee-en–ying | 叶剑英 |
| **Marshal Ye** | Yè shuài | yeh shwhy | 叶帅 |
| **Li Xiannian (Li Hsien-nien)** | Lǐ Xiānnián | lee shee-en–nee-en | 李先念 |
| **Chen Yun** | Chén Yún | chun yew-win | 陈云 |
| **Wang Dongxing** | Wáng Dōngxīng | wahng doong–sheeng | 汪东兴 |

| Hu Yaobang | Hú Yáobāng | hoo yao–bung | 胡耀邦 |
| Hu Qiaomu | Hú Qiáomù | hoo chee-ow–moo | 胡乔木 |
| Fang Yi | Fāng Yì | fahng yee | 方毅 |
| Song Qingling (Madame Sun Yat-sen) | Sòng Qìnglíng | soong ching–ling | 宋庆龄 |
| Deng Yingchao (Zhou Enlai's widow) | Dèng Yīngchāo | dung ying–chao | 邓颖超 |
| Liu Shaoqi | Liú Shàoqí | lee-oh shao–chee | 刘少奇 |
| Peng Dehuai | Pèng Déhuái | pung duh–hwhy | 彭德怀 |
| Yang Kaihui (Mao's second wife) | Yáng Kāihùi | young kye–hway | 杨开慧 |
| The Gang of Four | Sìrénbāng | suh–run–bung | 四人帮 |
| Wang Hongwen | Wáng Hóngwén | wahng hoong–win | 王洪文 |
| Zhang Chunqiao | Zhāng Chūnqiáo | jahng chwin–chee-ow | 张春桥 |
| Jiang Qing (Chiang Ch'ing) | Jiāng Qīng | jee-ahng ching | 江青 |
| Yao Wenyuan | Yáo Wényuán | yao win yoo-ahn | 姚文元 |
| Lin Biao | Lín Biāo | lin bee-ow | 林彪 |
| Chen Boda | Chén Bódá | chun baw–dah | 陈伯达 |
| Kang Sheng | Kāng Shēng | kung shung | 康生 |

## *HISTORICAL*

**Qin Shihuang**
(259–210 BC)
Emperor who unified China, founded
the Qin dynasty and built the Great Wall.

Qín Shǐhuáng    chin shir–hwahng    秦始皇

**Zhuge Liang**
(AD 181–234)
Major strategist of the Three Kingdoms
Period and popular hero.

Zhūgé Liàng    jew-guh lee-ung    诸葛亮

**Wu Zetian**
(624–705)
Empress during the Tang dynasty;
infamous for her corruption and
debauchery.

Wǔ Zétiān    woo dzih–tee-en    武则天

**Yue Fei**
(1103–42)
National hero of the Song dynasty,
betrayed by the traitor Qin Kuai.

Yuè Fēi    yweh–fay    岳飞

**Hong Xiuquan**
(1814–64)
Leader of the Taiping rebellion in South China. Deeply influenced by Christian thought and finally defeated by a united Chinese and foreign army.

Hóng Xiùquán

hoong shee-oh–chwan

洪秀全

**Kang Youwei**
(1858–1927)
Political reformer and advocate of constitutional monarchy.

Kāng Yŏuwéi

kung yo–way

康有为

**Liang Qichao**
(1873–1927)
Writer, editor and politician. Activist in the late Qing dynasty who advocated political reform.

Liáng Qǐchāo

lee-ahng chee–chee-ow

梁启超

**Cixi Taihou**
(1835–1908)
Empress Dowager and last effective ruler of the Qing dynasty. Her lavish and corrupt government saw the end of dynastic rule in China.

Cíxǐ Tàihòu

tsih–shee tye–hoe

慈禧太后

## CLASSICAL WRITERS

**Kong Zi (Confucius)** (551–479 BC)

Kóng Zǐ/ Kǒngfūzǐ

koongdzih/ koong–foodzih

孔子/ 孔夫子

Philosopher and politician of the Spring and Autumn Period. Apart from editing China's major classics, Confucius founded a school of philosophy. His sayings were collected in a book called *The Analects (Lunyu)*.

**Lao Zi (Laotse)** (5th century BC)

Laó Zǐ

laodzih

老子

Philosopher and founder of Taoism. Author of *The Way (Daodejing)*, a cryptic philosophical text.

**Meng Zi (Mengtse, Mencius)** (372–289 BC)

Mèng Zǐ

mung–dzih

孟子

Political philosopher and follower of Confucius.

**Zhuang Zi (Chuangtse)** (c 369–286 BC)

Zhuàng Zǐ

Zhwahng–dzih

庄子

Philosopher of the Warring States Period, author of *Zhuangzi* and follower of Lao Zi.

**Qu Yuan**
(c 340–278 BC)
China's first famous poet, and writer of
*Leaving Sorrow (Lisao)*, who also
served as a statesman.

Qū Yuán        chüyoo-en        屈原

**Sima Qian**
(c 143 BC)
Minister of the Eastern Han, author of
*The Chronicles of History (Shiji)*,
China's first major history and model
for all later works.

Sīmǎ Qiān      suh–mah chee-en  司马迁

**Xuan Zhuang**
(AD 602–664)
A Buddhist monk of the early Tang
dynasty who traveled to India to find
Buddhist scriptures. This trip later
became the theme for a popular
classical novel, *Journey to the West
(Xiyouji)*.

Xuán Zhuāng    shoo-en jew-ahng  玄装

**Li Bai**
(701–62)
Famous poet of the Tang dynasty.

Lǐ Bái         lee bye          李白

| | | | |
|---|---|---|---|
| **Du Fu**<br>(710–70)<br>Poet of the Tang dynasty noted for his realism. | Dù Fū | doo foo | 杜甫 |
| **Bai Juyi**<br>(772–846)<br>Tang dynasty poet. | Bái Jūyì | bye jü–yee | 白居易 |
| **So Dongpo (Su Shi)**<br>(1037–1101)<br>Poet and essayist of the Song dynasty. | Sū Dōngpō | soo dong–po | 苏东坡 |
| **Xing Qiji**<br>(1140–1207)<br>Poet and nationalist of the Song dynasty. | Xīng Qìjí | shing chee–jee | 辛弃疾 |
| **Cao Xueqin**<br>(c 1715–64)<br>Author of *Dream of Red Mansions (Hongloumeng)*, an epic novel describing the decline of a feudal Chinese family. | Cáo Xuěqín | tsao shoo-eh–cheen | 曹雪芹 |

**Guan Hanqing**     Guān Hànqīng     gwan han–ching     关汉卿
Yuan dramatist, known as "China's
Shakespeare."

## *MODERN WRITERS & ARTISTS*

**Lu Xun**     Lǔ Xùn     loo shwin     鲁迅
(1881–1936)
Novelist, essayist regarded as the
father of modern Chinese writing.

**Guo Moruo**     Guō Mòruò     gwaw moh–roo-waw     郭沫若
(1892–1978)
Poet and writer, leader in the modern
Chinese literary movement.

**Mao Dun**     Máo Dùn     mao dwin     茅盾
(1896–     )
Novelist and literary leader.

**Cao Yu**     Cáo Yú     tsao yü     曹禺
(1910–     )
Playwright and
critic.

**Ba Jin**
(1904–    )
Influential novelist, *The Family* being
his most famous story.

Bā Jīn          bah jeen          巴金

**Lao She**
(1899–1966)
Novelist, playwright, and humorist.

Láo Shě          lao sheh          老舍

**Ai Qing**
(1910–    )
Poet.

Aì Qīng          aye ching          艾青

**Ding Ling**
(1907–    )
China's most influential modern
woman writer.

Dīng Líng          ding ling          丁玲

**Wang Meng**
(1934–    )
An influential writer.

Wáng Měng          wahng mung          王蒙

**Ru Zhijuan**
(1925–    )
A woman writer.

Rú Zhìjuān          roo jir–jwan          茹志鹃

**Liu Xinwu**
(1942–    )
The most active post-1976 short-story writer in China.

Liú Xīnwŭ

lee-oh sheen–woo

刘心武

**Zhao Dan**
China's most popular male actor and male lead in numerous films.

Zhaò Dān

jao dan

赵丹

**Bai Yang**
A famous leading lady and actress, active in China's film industry since the 30's.

Bái Yáng

Bye yahng

白杨

**Qi Baishi**
(1864–1957)
An extremely influential painter whose works are very popular in China.

Qĭ Báishí

chee bye-shir

齐白石

**Wu Zuoren**
An artist versatile in traditional Chinese as well as Western painting.

Wŭ Zuòrén

wo dzwaw–run

吴作人

**Huang Yongyu**
The most popular contemporary painter.

Huáng Yŏngyù

hwahng yoong–yü

黄永玉

## OTHERS

**Li Shizen**
(1518–93)
A doctor of the Ming dynasty, author of one of China's major medical works. An expert in the use of herbal medicine.

Lǐ Shízēn     lee shir–juhn     李时珍

**Qian Xuesen**
China's main nuclear scientist.

Qián Xuésēn     chee-en shoo-eh–sun     钱学森

**Hua Luogeng**
A leading mathematician.

Huà Luógēng     hwa lwaw–gung     华罗庚

**Chen Jingrun**
A young mathematician of international repute.

Chén Jīngrùn     chun jing–rwun     陈景润

**Qian Sanqiang**
One of China's leading physicists.

Qián Sānqiáng     chee-en san–chee-ahng     钱三强

**Norman Bethune**
(1890–1939)
Canadian doctor who went to China during the Anti-Japanese War to help the Communist Party. Regarded as an internationalist hero in China.

Bái Qiú'ēn    bye chee-oh-en    白求恩

**Sun Wukong**
"Monkey," one of the most popular fictional characters in China, featured in the novel *Journey to the West* and in many operas and stories.

Sūn Wùkōng    swun woo-koong    孙悟空

**A Q**
A character in Lu Xun's short story *The True Story of A Q (A Q Zheng-zhuan)*, written in 1921. A Q is regarded as representing many of the faults of the Chinese character.

Ah Q    ah-cue    阿 Q

**Hou Baolin**
China's leading comic, performer of comic stage dialogue (*xiangsheng*).

Hòu Bǎolín    hoe bao-leen    侯宝林

| Kilogram | gōngjīn | goong–jeen | 公斤 |
| Catty | jīn (shìjīn) | jeen (shir–jeen) | 斤（市斤） |
| Pound | bàng | bung | 磅 |
| Milligram | gōngfēn/kè | goong–fun/kuh | 公分/克 |
| Liang | liǎng | lee-ahng | 两 |
| Ounce | ànshì | an–shir | 安士 |
| Kilometer | gōnglǐ | goong–lee | 公里 |
| Li | lǐ | lee | 里 |
| Mile | lǐ | lee | 哩 |
| Metre | mǐ | mee | 米 |
| Chinese foot | chǐ | chir | 尺 |
| Foot | chǐ | chir | 呎 |
| Millimeter | háomǐ | hao–mee | 毫米 |
| Chinese inch | cùn | tswin | 寸 |
| Inch | cùn | tswin | 吋 |
| Hectare | gōngqīng | goong–ching | 公顷 |
| Mou | mǔ (shìmǔ) | moo (shir–moo) | 亩/市亩 |
| Acre | yīngmǔ | ying–moo | 英亩 |

## ■ *WEIGHT COMPARISON TABLE*

1 kilogram = 2 catties = 2.205 pounds
1 catty = .5 kilograms = 1.102 pounds
1 pound = .454 kilograms = .907 catties

## ■ *DISTANCE*

1 kilometer = 2 li = .621 miles
1 li = .5 kilometers = .311 miles
1mile = 1.609 kilometers = 3.219 li
1 meter = 3 Chinese feet = 3.281 feet
1 Chinese foot = .333 meters = 1.094 feet
1 foot = .305 meters = .914 Chinese feet

## ■ *AREA*

1 hectare = 15 mou = 2.47 acres
1 mou = .065 hectares = .164 acres
1 acre = 0.405 hectares = 6:070 mou

# HOLIDAYS & FESTIVALS

**January** ❀ New Year (solar).

Late January or early February is the general time of the lunar New Year which fluctuates in its date on the Julian Calendar. This is the most important festival in the Chinese calendar and there are three days public holiday. It is a time when families reunite and universities have a winter holiday. The celebrations continue on the 2nd, 3rd and 4th days of the lunar New Year. This festival is called Spring Festival, or Chūnjié ( 春节 ) in Chinese.

**March 8** ❀ International Woman's Day (Fùnǚjié 妇女节 ).

Though not a public holiday special activities are organized for women on this day.

**April 5** ❀ Qingming Festival (Qīngmíngjié 清明节 ).

The Chinese All Saints day during which people visit their ancestors' graves and sweep them. It is now also a day of rememberance for martyrs of the revolution.

**May 1** ❀ Labor Day (Láodòngjié 劳动节 ).

Also called May 1 (Wǔ-yī, 五·一 ).

**May 4** ❀ Youth Festival (Qīngniánjié 青年节 ).

In commemoration of the student movement of May 4, 1919, or the May 4 Movement.

**May 30** ❀ Dragon Boat Festival (Duānwǔjié 端午节 ).

In commemoration of the loyal minister and poet Qu Yuan. Boats with dragon helms have races on rivers and lakes throughout the country and cakes are thrown into the water as a sacrifice to Qu.

**June 1** ❀ Children's Day (Ertongjié 儿童节 ).

**July 1** ❀ Anniversary of the founding of the Chinese Communist Party.

**August 1** ❀ Anniversary of the founding of the People's Liberation Army.

This marks the date of the Nanchang Uprising in 1927 which saw the creation of the Red Army, later renamed the People's Liberation Army (P.L.A.)

**October 1** ❀ National Day.

Commemoration of the founding of the People's Republic of China in 1949. This is a national holiday, in Chinese it is called Guóqìng ( 国庆 ) or Shíyī ( 十·一 , lit., "the first of October").

**October 6** ❀ Mid-Autumn Festival (Zhōngqiūjié 中秋节 ).

A traditional festival marking the harvest. Moon-cakes (yuèbǐng 月饼 ) are eaten and people sit outside during the night to look at the moon.

**October 29** ❀ Chongyang Festival (Chóngyángjié 重阳节 ).

The ninth day of the ninth month of the lunar calendar, therefore also called Double Nine Festival (Chóngjiūjié 重九节 ).

**Note:** National holidays consist of one day at New Year, three days at the Chinese New Year, and one day each for Labor Day and National Day.

# *CHRONOLOGY*
## *OF CHINESE DYNASTIES & REPUBLICS*

| | | | |
|---|---|---|---|
| **Xia Dynasty** 夏朝 | | | c 21st–16th centuries BC |
| **Shang Dynasty** 商朝 | | | c 16th century–1066 BC |
| **Zhou Dynasty** 周朝 | Western Zhou 西周 | | c 1066–771 BC |
| | Eastern Zhou 东周 | | 770–256 BC |
| | Spring and Autumn Period 春秋时代 | | 772–481 BC |
| | Warring States Period 战国时代 | | 403–221 BC |
| **Qin Dynasty** 秦朝 | | | 221–206 BC |
| **Han Dynasty** 汉朝 | Western Han 西汉 | | 206 BC–AD 23 |
| | Eastern Han 东汉 | | AD 25–220 |
| **Three Kingdoms Period** 三国时代 | State of Wei 魏国 | | 220–65 |
| | State of Shu 蜀国 | | 221–63 |
| | State of Wu 吴国 | | 222–80 |
| **Western Jin Dynasty** 西晋 | | | 265–316 |

| | | |
|---|---|---|
| **Eastern Jin & Sixteen States** 东晋十六国 | Eastern Jin 东晋 | 317–420 |
| | Sixteen States 十六国 | 304–439 |
| **South and North Dynasties** 南北朝 | SOUTH DYNASTIES 南朝 | |
| | Song 宋 | 420–79 |
| | Qi 齐 | 479–502 |
| | Liang 梁 | 502–57 |
| | Chen 陈 | 557–89 |
| | NORTH DYNASTIES 北朝 | |
| | Northern Wei 北魏 | 386–534 |
| | Eastern Wei 西魏 | 534–50 |
| | Northern Qi 北齐 | 550–77 |
| | Western Wei 西魏 | 535–57 |
| | Northern Zhou 北周 | 557–81 |
| **Sui Dynasty** 隋朝 | | 581–618 |
| **Tang Dynasty** 唐朝 | | 618–907 |
| **Five Dynasties and Ten Kingdoms Period** 五代十国 | Later Liang 后梁 | 907–23 |
| | Later Tang 后唐 | 923–36 |
| | Later Jin 后晋 | 936–46 |

| | | | | |
|---|---|---|---|---|
| | Later Han | 后汉 | 后周 | 947–50 |
| | Later Zhou | | | 951–60 |
| | Ten Kingdoms | 十国 | | 902–79 |
| **Song Dynasty** 宋朝 | Northern Song | 北宋 | | 960–1127 |
| | Southern Song | | 南宋 | 1127–1279 |
| **Liao (Kitan) Dynasty** 辽代 | | | | 907–1125 |
| **Western Xia** 西夏 | | | | 1032–1227 |
| **Jin (Nurchen) Dynasty** 金代 | | | | 1115–1234 |
| **Yuan (Mongol) Dynasty** 元朝 | | | | 1279–1368 |
| **Ming Dynasty** 明朝 | | | | 1368–1644 |
| **Qing (Manchu) Dynasty** 清朝 | | | | 1644–1911 |
| **Republic of China** 中华民国 | | | | 1912–1949 |
| **People's Republic of China** 中华人民共和国 | | | | 1949– |

## GEOGRAPHICAL FEATURES

| East China Sea | Dōng Hǎi | 东海 |
| South China Sea | Nán Hǎi | 南海 |
| Yangtse River | Cháng Jiāng | 长江 |
| Yellow River | Huáng Hé | 黄河 |

## PROVINCES & AUTONOMOUS REGIONS

| Anhwei | Ānhuī | 安徽省 |
| Chekiang | Zhèjiāng | 浙江 |
| Fukien | Fújiàn | 福建 |
| Heilungkiang | Hēilóngjiāng | 黑龙江 |
| Honan | Hénán | 河南 |
| Hopei | Héběi | 河北 |
| Hunan | Húnán | 湖南 |
| Hupei (Hupeh) | Húběi | 湖北 |
| Inner Mongolia Aut. Reg. | Neì Ménggǔ Zìzhìqū | 内蒙古自治区 |

**PLACE NAMES**

| Kansu | Gānsù | 甘肃 |
| Kiangsi | Jiāngxī | 江西 |
| Kirin | Jílín | 吉林 |
| Kwangsi Aut. Reg. | Guǎngxī Zhuàngzú Zìzhìqū | 广西壮族自治区 |
| Kwangtung | Guǎngdōng | 广东 |
| Kweichow | Guìzhōu | 贵州 |
| Liaoning | Liáoníng | 辽宁 |
| Ningsia Hui Aut. Reg. | Níngxià Huízú Zìzhìqū | 宁夏回族自治区 |
| Shansi | Shānxī | 山西 |
| Shantung | Shāndōng | 山东 |
| Shensi | Shǎnxī | 陕西 |
| Sinkiang Uighur Aut. Reg. | Xīngjiāng Wéiwúěr Zìzhìqū | 新疆维吾尔自治区 |
| Szechwan | Sìchuān | 四川 |
| Taiwan | Táiwān | 台湾 |
| Tibet Aut. Reg. | Xīzàng Zìzhìqū | 西藏自治区 |
| Tsinghai | Qīnghǎi | 青海 |
| Yunnan | Yúnnán | 云南 |

## CITIES & LOCALITIES

| | | |
|---|---|---|
| Anshan | Ānshān | 鞍山 |
| Changchun | Chángchūn | 长春 |
| Changsha | Chángshā | 长沙 |
| Chengchow | Zhèngzhōu | 郑州 |
| Chengtu | Chéngdū | 成都 |
| Chungking | Chóngqìng | 重庆 |
| Hangchow | Hángzhōu | 杭州 |
| Harbin | Hā'ěrbīn | 哈尔滨 |
| Huhehot | Hūhéhàotè | 呼和浩特 |
| Kunming | Kūnmíng | 昆明 |
| Kwangchow (Canton) | Guǎngzhōu | 广州 |
| Kweilin | Guìlín | 桂林 |
| Loyang | Luòyáng | 洛阳 |
| Nanking | Nánjīng | 南京 |
| Nanning | Nánníng | 南宁 |
| Peking | Běijīng | 北京 |
| Shanghai | Shànghǎi | 上海 |

| | | |
|---|---|---|
| Shaoshan | Shàoshān | 韶山 |
| Shenyang | Shěnyàng | 沈阳 |
| Shih Chia Chuang | Shìjiāzhuāng | 石家庄 |
| Sian | Xī'ān | 西安 |
| Soochow | Sūzhōu | 苏州 |
| Tachai | Dàzhài | 大寨 |
| Taching | Dàqìng | 大庆 |
| Talien | Dàlián | 大连 |
| Tatung | Dàtóng | 大同 |
| Tientsin | Tiānjīn | 天津 |
| Tsinan | Jìnán | 济南 |
| Tsingtao | Qīngdǎo | 青岛 |
| Urumchi | Wūlūmùqī | 乌鲁木齐 |
| Wuhan | Wǔhàn | 武汉 |
| Wuhsi | Wúxī | 无锡 |
| Yenan | Yán'ān | 延安 |

**About Chinese**, Richard Newnham. Penguin, 1971.

**Chinese Characters**, L. Weiger, S.J. New York: Dover Publications, 1965.

**Elementary Chinese**. Part I (with 4 tapes), Peking: Commercial Press, 1975; Part II (with 4 tapes), Peking: Commercial Press, 1972.

**The Chinese Language**, Bernhard Karlgren. Ronald Press, 1949.

**Language and Linguistics in the People's Republic of China**, Winfred P. Lehmann, ed. Austin: Univ. of Texas Press, 1975.

**Language Reform in China**, Peter Seybolt and Gregory Chiang, eds. White Plains, N.Y.: M.E. Sharpe, 1979.

**Reading and Writing Chinese**, William McNaughton. Rutland: Charles E. Tuttle, Co., 1979.

**Sound and Symbol in Chinese**, Bernhard Karlgren. Hong Kong and Oxford, rev. edn. 1962.

## DICTIONARIES

**The Chinese-English Dictionary**, Peking Foreign Languages Institute. Hong Kong: Commercial Press, 1979.

**An English-Chinese Dictionary**. Shanghai: Joint Publishing (Hong Kong), 1976.

# NOTES

# NOTES

# NOTES